Contents

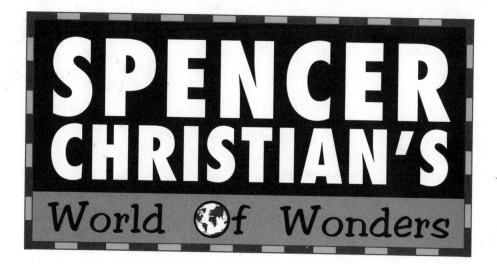

Spencer Christian's World Of Wonders

Can It Really Rain Frogs?

THE WORLD'S STRANGEST WEATHER EVENTS

Spencer Christian
and Antonia Felix

JOHN WILEY & SONS, INC.

New York • Chichester • Weinheim • Brisbane • Singapore • Toronto

Copyright © 1997 by Spencer Christian and Antonia Felix.
Published by John Wiley & Sons, Inc.
Design by Pronto Design & Production Inc.
Illustrations: Abe Blashko for the illustrations of Spencer Christian and the illustrations on pages 37, 41, 55, 81, 90, and 91 and Jessica Wolk-Stanley for the other illustrations.

Library of Congress Cataloging-in-Publication Data
Christian, Spencer.
    Can it really rain frogs?: the world's strangest weather events / Spencer Christian and Antonia Felix.
        p.   cm — (Spencer Christian's world of wonders)
    Includes index.
    Summary: Describes strange weather events such as raining frogs, singing caves, colored rain, and auroras, and discusses weather lore and weather forecasting.
    ISBN 0-471-15290-0 (pbk. : alk. paper)
    1. Weather—Juvenile literature. 2. Meteorology—Juvenile literature. [1. Weather. 2. Meteorology.] I. Felix, Antonia. II. Title III. Series: Christian, Spencer. Spencer Christian's world of wonders.
    QC981.3.C5 1997   96-47735
    551.5–dc21

Printed in the United States of America
10 9 8 7 6 5 4 3 2 1

Introduction

WELCOME TO THE WONDERS OF WEATHER

Weather is the number one topic all over the world.

As long as human beings have been on Earth, we have been affected by the weather. We get frustrated by storms that interrupt our travel or picnic plans, and we take great pleasure in the warm, early days of spring and the gentle rains that make the flowers bloom. All over the world, weather is one thing that everyone is interested in.

In this book, we'll look at many fascinating and even **bizarre** facts about the weather. We'll explore the big picture, such as the atmosphere and Earth's water system, and we'll uncover interesting details like the dazzling variety of snowflakes and the makeup of a lightning bolt. We'll discover the awesome power of wild winds in hurricanes and tornadoes. Can a groundhog really predict how many more months of winter are in store? We'll look at this popular tradition and much more weather folklore. And we'll learn that throughout history, there have been strange and downright wacky weather reports of showers that have poured down everything from clams and spiders to a *human* hailstone and—yes—frogs!

Although I haven't been lucky enough to report a frog shower in my career as a weather forecaster (not yet, anyway), my life has been filled with many exciting and even frightening experiences with weather. I'll share these stories with you as together we discover the wild and wonderful world of weather.

1

Meet the Wild and Wonderful World Weather Machine

Weather is the sum of the outdoor conditions we face every day, such as rain, snow, wind, and clouds. Without wind and clouds, the sun would bake the area near the equator to temperatures close to the boiling point of water, while much of the rest of our planet would be bitterly cold. Without rain, all land areas would be dust and rock incapable of supporting plants, animals, or people.

So, our planet is lucky to have weather—and lots of it. The 𝕒𝕨𝕖𝕤𝕠𝕞𝕖 processes that created our planet also created a system that I like to call the great world weather machine. Before we go on to the details of weather, we'll explore the fascinating workings of this wonderful machine.

🌐 Weather is what happens outside our windows every day, while **climate** is the pattern of weather that occurs over long periods of time.

The Sun

All of Earth's energy comes from our sun, which, like every other star in the universe, is really a gigantic nuclear reactor. At the center of this giant ball of gases, 600 million metric tons of hydrogen are burned every second, creating temperatures up to 36 million° Fahrenheit (2.2 million° Celsius). At its surface, the sun's temperature is a toasty 11,000° Fahrenheit (6,093° Celsius), and a patch the size of a postage stamp gives off enough energy to light five hundred 60-watt light bulbs. Although only a small amount of the sun's energy hits Earth, it provides as much heat as burning 700 billion tons of coal per day.

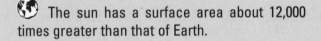

🌐 The sun has a surface area about 12,000 times greater than that of Earth.

How Earth Takes the Heat

Like the energy from a fireplace, the heat from the sun doesn't warm all parts of our planet evenly. A much larger portion of the sun's energy is absorbed by the area north and south of the equator that we call the **tropics**. The **equator** is the imaginary circle around the earth that divides the Northern Hemisphere, the top half, from the Southern Hemisphere, the bottom half. If there were no way to distribute the sun's heat more evenly, temperatures near the equator would average 130° to 140° Fahrenheit (54°–60° Celsius)!

On the other hand, most of the rest of the world would have an **arctic** climate, and the harbors of cities like New York and Sydney, Australia, would be clogged with ice every day of the year.

Instead, including the tropics, there are five climate zones on Earth. **Temperate** climates are regions that have warm summers, cold winters, and rain and snow. **Desert** climates have hot and dry weather throughout the year. **Arctic** climates, also called polar climates, are the coldest on Earth, and occur near the North and South Poles. Areas with subarctic climates have long, cold winters, light snow, and cool summers.

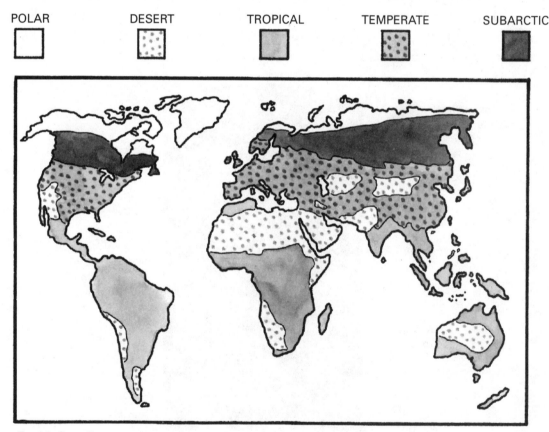

POLAR DESERT TROPICAL TEMPERATE SUBARCTIC

Earth's five climate zones

Why are there so many different climates on Earth? The answer has to do with air, water, and weather. Air and water are the basis of our planet's heating and cooling system. Let's take a look at our planet's oceans of air and water, and discover how they move around to transfer heat.

The Atmosphere

Picture Earth as you've seen it in photographs taken from space—a blue ball covered with swirls of white clouds. The beautiful blue color is caused by sunlight reflecting off Earth's **atmosphere**. Now imagine this ball the size of a schoolroom globe. How big would our model Earth be if it also showed the atmosphere, the life-giving layer of gases that surrounds the planet? The change would be almost impossible to notice, because the atmosphere would appear as a layer about as thick as a coat of clear varnish. This layer appears very thin from space, but it contains our entire life-support system—all our weather and protection from the sun's radiation.

Although small traces of our atmosphere can be found hundreds of miles from Earth, almost all of it is pressed into a layer that extends **6 miles** (10 kilometers) up from the surface. This layer of atmosphere is called the **troposphere**,

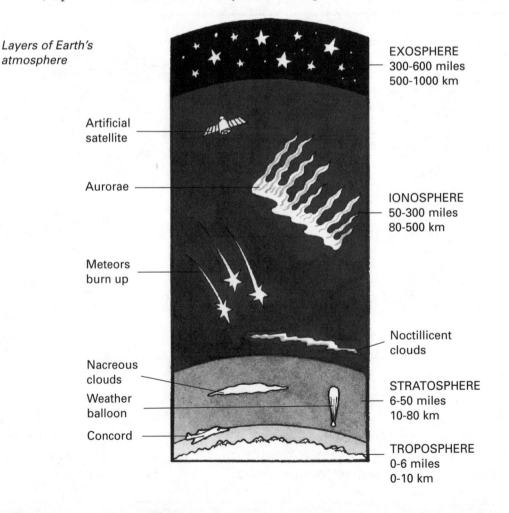

Layers of Earth's atmosphere

Artificial satellite

Aurorae

Meteors burn up

Nacreous clouds

Weather balloon

Concord

EXOSPHERE
300-600 miles
500-1000 km

IONOSPHERE
50-300 miles
80-500 km

Noctillicent clouds

STRATOSPHERE
6-50 miles
10-80 km

TROPOSPHERE
0-6 miles
0-10 km

and it is here that weather occurs. The next level, the **stratosphere**, extends to 50 miles (80 kilometers) above the planet. The **ionosphere** is the next level, 50 to 300 miles (80 to 500 kilometers) above Earth. When you see a falling star, a meteor burning up in the atmosphere, you're looking into the ionosphere. Beyond that is the **exosphere** and, you guessed it, space—the final frontier.

The atmosphere is made up of gases that are constantly on the move. Most of these gases were created within Earth itself over millions of years. When our planet was very young, volcanoes exploded huge amounts of poisonous gases into the air. When plants developed in the sea and on land, they began releasing oxygen into the atmosphere. The air you are breathing right now is the product of plants that lived millions of years ago!

Air is a mixture of invisible molecules of nitrogen, oxygen, carbon dioxide, water vapor, and a few other substances. These molecules are kept from flying off into space by **gravity**, the force that attracts objects to Earth.

Air is a very mysterious substance. If you open and close your hand, it feels like nothing is there. But when you breath, something substantial fills your lungs. While air seems weightless when you hold a balloon, under pressure it fills tires that can support the weight of huge trucks. Although it seems harmless on a calm day, in violent storms moving air can topple trees, demolish buildings, and even pick up railroad cars and carry them hundreds of yards.

Your body is not affected by air pressure in the atmosphere because the pressure inside your body balances the pressure outside.

What Is Air Pressure?

Although air is about 800 times less dense than water, the total weight of the air surrounding Earth comes to 5.75 quadrillion tons. That translates into a weight of about 14.7 pounds (6.6 kilograms) on every square inch, or about 1 ton (.91 metric tons) of weight on your entire body.

Why don't you feel it? Put your palms together in front of your chest and push. Your hands don't move because the force pushing from both directions is equal. You don't feel **air pressure** because there is pressure inside your body as well as outside, so the forces are equal. However, when you go up in an airplane or elevator, air trapped inside your ears has a higher pressure than the air outside your body. The pressure of the air pushing out makes your ears "pop," equalizing the pressure.

There are lots of other examples of how air reacts under pressure. When you blow up a balloon, you force air inside, increasing the pressure. If you push on the surface of the balloon, you can feel the high-pressure air inside pushing back. Puncture the balloon, and the air rushes out with a force you can feel. The more tightly air is packed, the stronger the force.

In a low-pressure system, air rises and cools to form clouds and sometimes precipitation. Air under high pressure sinks, creating clear skies.

DO-IT-YOURSELF WEATHER-WATCHING: THE BAROMETER

The weather instrument used to measure air pressure is called a **barometer**. You can observe changes in air pressure yourself with your own homemade barometer.

What You Need:
- Balloon
- Scissors
- Wide-mouthed glass jar
- Rubber band
- Toothpick
- Glue
- Tape
- Pencil
- 3" x 5" index card, or piece of paper cut to that size

What to Do:

1. Cut off the neck of the balloon, and stretch the rest of the balloon over the mouth of the clean, dry jar.
2. Secure the balloon in place with the rubber band.
3. Glue the toothpick onto the top of the balloon, with half of it sticking over the edge of the jar.
4. Position the card on the jar so the toothpick points to the center, and attach with tape. Draw a short line at this center point, and two lines above and two lines below it. Write the word "High" above the toothpick, and "Low" below the toothpick.
5. Place the barometer indoors, away from windows, where it will not be affected by moisture or heat. Observe the barometer daily, and note the changes on a sheet of paper. What kind of weather occurs one or two days after the toothpick moves to the "Low" area?

What Happens and Why:

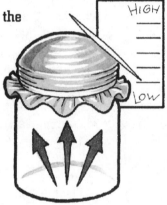

The air pressure inside your jar stays the same, but the air outside changes. When the air pressure outside increases, it pushes down on the balloon surface. This causes the toothpick to point upward, into the "High" area. When the air pressure outside decreases, the pressure inside is stronger. The higher air pressure inside the jar pushes out against the balloon surface. This makes the toothpick point downward, toward "Low." A low air-pressure reading tells you that warm air is rising and cooling, forming clouds that can bring rain. A high-pressure reading predicts fair, dry weather.

Naming the Wind

In 50 B.C., the great Roman general Julius Caesar commissioned a Greek architect to construct a magnificent eight-sided, 46-foot-high white tower in the center of Athens. Why eight sides? This building was called the Tower of the Winds, because each side represented a direction from which the wind blew: north, northeast, east, southeast, and so on. On each side was carved a sculpture that showed the nature of the wind that came from that direction. For example, North was represented by a man dressed in warm clothes, to show that the wind from the north was cold, and West was a man carrying a flowerpot, to show that the west wind carried warmth.

Today, we still label the winds according to the direction from which they come. For example, when the weather forecaster announces that there is a 10-mile-per-hour northwest wind, it means the wind is blowing *from* the northwest.

How Does Air Pressure Get Things Moving?

Many weather events are related to air pressure. Air pressure varies from place to place on our planet. Cold, heavy air sinks closer to Earth and causes an increase in air pressure. But warm, light air tends to rise, reducing air pressure. When cold air sinks down, it squeezes the warm air beneath it away. That is why, at ground level, the winds blow from cold places to warm places. When air moves straight up and down, we call it a **current**. When it moves **horizontally**, we call it wind.

Measuring changes in air pressure is a good way of predicting weather. High air pressure is a sign of fair weather, but if air pressure drops sharply, there's a good chance of rain or a storm.

Where the Winds Blow

The winds move air all around the planet, bringing warmer air to cooler areas and cooler air to warmer areas. Because the temperature in different levels of the atmosphere is not always the same, winds high above the ground can blow in a direction that is different from the directions of winds at the surface. Some winds blow in the same general direction all year long, while others blow in certain seasons, at certain times of the day, or only when storms arise.

There are four basic types of winds: prevailing winds, seasonal winds, local winds, and storm winds.

Prevailing winds

Although the weather changes from day to day, the equator is always hot and the poles are always cold. As a result of this fundamental temperature difference, Earth is ringed by bands of winds that generally blow in the same direction. These **prevailing winds** are the most important part of the system that moderates the temperatures on our planet.

- The equatorial **doldrums**: The area near the equator receives so much sunshine that the hot air rises almost straight upwards in strong currents, so there is very little wind.

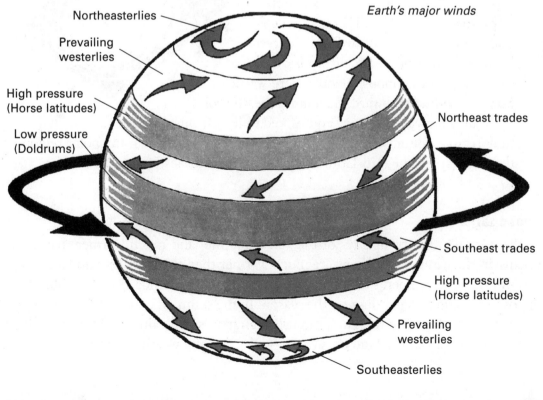

Earth's major winds

Northeasterlies

Prevailing westerlies

High pressure (Horse latitudes)

Low pressure (Doldrums)

Northeast trades

Southeast trades

High pressure (Horse latitudes)

Prevailing westerlies

Southeasterlies

- The northeast trade winds: When the warm air around the equator rises, cooler air moves towards the equator to replace it. Because Earth spins faster near the equator, the movement of air flows northeast from the coast of Africa towards the Caribbean Sea. These winds are called the **trade winds** because in the early years of ocean travel, ships used their power to reach distant places where goods could be traded.
- The horse latitudes: At about 30 degrees north and south latitudes, the air that was warmed near the equator cools and sinks straight downward, producing a narrow band of high pressure in which little wind blows. Many early sailing ships, caught in this band for weeks at a time, were forced to dump extra cargo, including horses, to make the vessel lighter. That's why this band is called the **horse latitudes**.
- The prevailing westerlies: The warm air that sinks in the horse latitudes is drawn toward the colder North and South Poles. This air, set in motion by the spinning of Earth, produces a broad band of winds blowing from west to east that covers almost all of the United States and Europe in the Northern Hemisphere, and the southern tip of South America, southern Australia, and New Zealand in the Southern Hemisphere.
- The polar easterlies—northeasterlies and southeasterlies: As warm air flows northward toward the North Pole, the cold polar air is drawn southward and is curved by Earth's rotation to flow from northeast to southwest. At the opposite end, where warm air is flowing southward toward the South Pole, the cold polar air is drawn northward and curved to flow from southeast to northwest. Because temperature differences are smaller in the polar regions than they are in the mid-latitudes, these polar easterlies tend to be weaker.

Seasonal winds

In the summer, the strong rays of the sun make the land much warmer than the oceans; in the winter, the oceans are much warmer than the land. In many areas of the world, these temperature differences mean that the winds generally blow in opposite directions depending on the season. In the summer, cooler, moist air from the water is blown over the land, often bringing seasonal rain. In the winter, the cooler air flows from the land toward the water, and the weather is much drier.

Local winds—land and sea breezes

The breezes that blow across the coast in tropical areas are called local winds. You can always count on them—the same wind pattern is repeated every day and every night. During the day, the wind blows from sea to land, and is called a sea breeze. As the sunshine heats up the land, the warm air over the land rises. Then the cool air from the sea is drawn in to replace it. The night brings a land breeze, when air moves from land to sea. After sundown, the sea stays warmer than the land, and as the air rises above it, cooler air from the land is drawn toward the sea.

Wind: The Incredible Mover and Shaper

We have never invented a machine as powerful as the wind, which helps to completely change Earth's surface every few million years. Here are some ways that wind alters the planet's shape:

Desert winds pound boulders into sand and dust.

Sand dunes are built up by desert winds that blow from one direction over a long period of time. Some dunes, reaching several stories high, slowly move across the desert landscape. In Iran and Algeria, some become as tall as skyscrapers!

Seeds carried by the wind take root and grow into plants and trees, which change the landscape wherever they grow.

In the Sahara Desert in northern Africa, very strong winds have lifted up and carried away rock to leave a huge, deep hole called the Qattara Depression.

A desert wind can act like a sculptor, creating interesting shapes as it blasts away at rock. In a process called **abrasion**, the wind carries away soft rock and leaves only the hard rock behind. A large area of hard, flat rock that has been worn down by abrasion is called a **plateau**. A mini-plateau, such as those found in Monument Valley, Arizona, is called a **mesa**.

Storm winds

Storm winds, such as those in tornadoes and hurricanes, are caused by special weather conditions. We'll learn much more about these later in the book.

Famous Winds

The windiest place on Earth: Commonwealth Bay, Antarctica, with gale winds that average 200 miles per hour (mph)

The most powerful wind ever recorded: 231 miles per hour (mph) at the top of Mount Washington in New Hampshire on April 12, 1934

Global Winds and the Spinning Planet

Earth's rotation has an important influence on global winds. We don't notice that Earth spins on its axis because we're attached to it, along with houses, trees, automobiles, and so forth. But the atmosphere isn't attached to the ground, which is constantly rotating out from under it.

If you stand on a piece of land on the equator, you are traveling about **1,000 miles per hour** to complete one 24-hour rotation. But if you're bundled up in your finest snowsuit near one of the poles, you're traveling much more slowly to rotate once in that same 24-hour period. This difference in speed in the rotation of the earth has an effect on anything flying over the surface, like wind. It causes the wind itself to rotate, and is called the **Coriolis effect**, after the name of the scientist who discovered it. Because of the Coriolis effect, groups of storm clouds in the Northern Hemisphere rotate in a counterclockwise direction, and storm systems in the Southern Hemisphere rotate clockwise.

The Jet Stream

n the 1940s, during the early days of World War II, American military commanders decided to send a small group of planes on a daring mission to bomb Tokyo, Japan. After a long, lonely flight over the Pacific, these planes climbed to a height of 30,000 feet to avoid antiaircraft fire. As the pilots turned their planes toward the east to make their bombing runs, they were astonished to notice that the speed of the planes soared to over 450 miles per hour, far beyond any speed they had been able to obtain before. These pilots had stumbled onto a high-level wind roaring from west to east at a speed of more than 150 miles per hour. Meteorologists soon discovered that this narrow band of strong upper level winds circled the entire globe. They called it the **jet stream**.

The jet stream is caused by the **clash** of warm air and cold air high in the clouds. When the temperature differences are strong, the wind's speed can be as high as 340 miles per hour. The jet stream is so powerful that it steers weather systems from west toward the east. The path and the direction of the jet stream changes with the location of warm and cold air masses. For example, if it dips south in the winter, cold polar air follows; when it swings back north, it brings warm, moist air along with it.

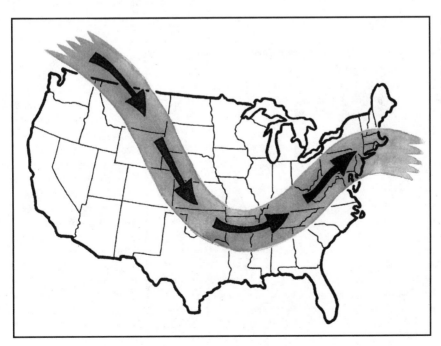

The jet stream is a fast-moving river of air flowing west to east several miles above Earth's surface.

Earth's Oceans

If an observer from another galaxy were to drop by to catalog our solar system, Earth probably would be described as the "water planet." Nearly three-quarters of our planet's surface (71 percent) is covered by oceans. These oceans play a critical role in maintaining a climate and environment that allow the life on Earth to exist and thrive. Ocean currents transfer heat northward from the regions near the equator and cold southward from the poles. The oceans also supply the vast amount of moisture needed to support life on land.

The Water Cycle

How water got into the sky to fall as rain was a big mystery to ancient civilizations. One belief was that rain gods opened up hidden streams in the skies. By the seventeenth century, the best explanation scientists could come up with was that liquid water somehow formed tiny little hollow bubbles that floated upward invisibly until they "popped" and dropped their water back to Earth.

Now we know that water can become a gas known as **water vapor**. This happens when water molecules move so fast that they break free of other molecules

In Earth's water cycle, water evaporates from the ocean, making the air moist. Air that moves over land and rises over high land is cooled. The rising, cool air forms clouds from which rain or snow may fall. The rain or snow runs into streams or rivers that eventually return the water to the ocean.

and escape into the air. Because this process requires energy, it happens as the temperature warms.

Although we don't see it happen, vast quantities of the water in the oceans **evaporates**, or changes into vapor, during the course of a year. At any given time, the air holds enough water to drop an inch of rain on every square inch of the planet. Most of it falls back into the oceans as rain. But a significant portion is blown over land and falls as rain or snow.

For more than **3 billion years**, Earth has been using the same water, recycling it from the oceans to the sky and back again. This process is called the **water cycle**. Sunlight heats the surface of the water in the oceans. This heat makes the water evaporate, and this moist air moves over land, cooling as it rises. This rising, cooling air forms clouds that produce rain. The rain flows into streams and rivers, and eventually back into the ocean. Earth's great water cycle plays a part in many types of weather that we'll be looking at throughout this book.

Ocean Currents

Global winds and wind systems account for about two-thirds of the heat transfer that makes so much of our planet livable. The other one-third is carried out by ocean currents, great rivers of water driven by temperature differences and the wind. Warm water from the tropics is blown northwestward by the prevailing winds and curved by the rotation of Earth. Eventually, this water cools, sinks, and flows back toward the equator to be warmed again.

One of the Earth's most important ocean currents is the **Gulf Stream**. This current begins near the equator off the coast of Africa and is blown by the trade winds towards the Caribbean along the path used by Christopher Columbus. It flows into the Gulf of Mexico, then back out off the coast of Florida and hugs the eastern coast of the United States until it reaches North Carolina. Then it splits, with one fork going eastward toward England and one going northeastward toward Iceland. This warm water has a tremendous effect on the climate of England, which is as far north as Canada's Hudson Bay, but not nearly as cold. Without the Gulf Stream, London would be icebound nearly all year; with the Gulf Stream, London's climate is more moderate than that of New York City.

In the Pacific, however, the warm water flows westward away from the United States coast. It is replaced by a current of cold water sweeping down from the north. This is why the weather in the Pacific Northwest is cool and damp much of the year.

Reading the Sky

THE SECRETS OF CLOUDS

Pretend you're a magician performing your most dazzling trick from the stage of a packed theater. You carefully measure a half cup of water, hold it out in front of you for your audience to see, mumble a few magic words, then suddenly— **POOF!** In an instant, the water expands to fill the entire theater with a thick white mist. The theater doors swing open and the mist drifts outside. As it reaches the street, it begins to rise. A moment later, the water magically reappears—as a brief, gentle rain.

Billions of times per day nature performs this amazing trick to produce the majestic riders of the sky that we call clouds.

What Is a Cloud?

A **cloud** is made up of tiny droplets of water or particles of ice suspended in the air. These droplets or particles are so small that it takes between 1 and 15 million of them to make a single raindrop. Have you ever gone for a walk on a foggy day? If you have, you've walked in a cloud—**fog** is just a cloud that touches the ground. Although the fog makes it harder to see, you can't touch it and it doesn't feel different than normal air.

Water Vapor

Clouds form from **water vapor**, water in a gas form that's part of all the air we breathe.

Hot air holds a lot more water vapor than cold air. When air is heated, it absorbs more water, like a sponge. When you cool air, it's like squeezing the sponge—water vapor becomes liquid water. For example, when you put ice cubes into a glass on a warm day, the outside of the glass becomes wet. That's because the air near the glass cools and cannot hold as much water vapor. We use the word **condensation** to describe water vapor turning into liquid water.

How Much Water Does a Cloud Hold?

A piece of a cloud that's the size of an average living room contains about 1 ounce of water. A typical cumulus cloud that dots the sky in fair weather and measures a few hundred yards across—your basic, ordinary cloud—contains only about 25 gallons (95 liters) of water. However, a puffy cumulus cloud that is 1/2 mile (.8 kilometers) square and as tall as it is wide holds about 58,000 pounds (26,300 kilograms) of water—the weight of twenty-five automobiles.

LET'S GET IN A FOG

When water vapor in the air cools and condenses, it forms mist. Spreading out over low-lying areas of land, mist is called fog. Let's create these tiny drops of liquid water and see condensation in action.

What You Need:
- Rolling pin
- Spoon
- Towel
- 1 cup salt
- 3 cups crushed ice cubes
- Deep mixing bowl or saucepan

What to Do:
1. Using about six ice cubes at a time, wrap the cubes in a towel and crush them with the rolling pin.
2. Pour the crushed ice into the bowl or pan.
3. Add the salt and stir.
4. Count to 100, or watch the clock and wait about 2 minutes.
5. Bring the bowl close to your face, and blow softly over the ice/salt mixture. It's mist!

What Happens and Why:
The ice in the bowl makes the surrounding air very cold. Your breath contains water vapor, and when it passes over the cold air, the water vapor condenses and creates mist. The salt reacts with the ice to make it melt in a special way. The melted saltwater stays near the freezing temperature (32° Fahrenheit, 0° Celsius). This keeps the air around the ice very cold—colder than it would be without the help of salt. The experiment works best in very cold air.

Clouds form in three ways: when air meets a mountain and is forced to rise and cool; when the air is heated on a hot summer day; and when a cold air mass meets a warm air mass, making the warm air rise and cool.

How Does Water Vapor Become a Cloud?

Clouds form in three basic ways:

- Air is forced upward when it runs into mountains. That's why mountain peaks are often shrouded by clouds.
- The sun heats the air over a certain area and the warmed air rises like steam escaping from a teakettle. This kind of heating causes thunderstorms on a hot, humid summer day. (When it is humid, there is a lot of moisture in the air.)
- A cold air mass collides with a warm air mass. As we learned in chapter 1, cold air is heavier than warm air, so when the two air masses meet, the cold air acts like a wedge and forces the warm air upward.

Many tall mountaintops are covered by snow even in the middle of the summer because the air temperature falls the higher you go above Earth's surface. It can be 50° to 60° colder at the top of a 20,000-foot-high mountain than at the base. When scientists of about 200 years ago discovered this, they decided that clouds form in the sky when warm air rises into the colder air and some of its water vapor condenses. But when they conducted scientific tests to prove their theory, they were shocked to find out that sometimes water vapor wouldn't condense no matter how cold the temperature got.

Finally, a French scientist named Paul Jean Coulier solved the puzzle. The secret of cloud formation was—dust! Every single cloud droplet condenses around an extremely tiny particle (the biggest are just one-tenth the width of one human hair). If air is perfectly clean, it is impossible for a cloud to form.

The Rain Forest Needs the Desert!

The size of the rain forests in South America is directly related to the size of Africa's Sahara Desert! The larger the desert, the more tiny particles of sand are blown all the way across the Atlantic Ocean. The more particles over South America, the more rain clouds form and the more moisture falls as rain to help the rain forests grow.

Where do these particles come from? Many types of windblown particles float in the air: salt from seawater, volcanic ash, debris from the impacts of meteors, pollen, plant spores, smoke, and dust. Most of these bits are very, very small—tinier than the specks of dust you see in a sunbeam when you clean your room.

What Are the Different Types of Clouds?

Growing up in central Virginia, my younger brother and I loved to watch the clouds and the moving shadows they cast on the countryside. Learning the basic types of clouds makes cloud-gazing a lot of fun, and in this chapter we'll cover everything from your basic, harmless fluffy cumulus cloud to rare, bizarre clouds that are not often seen.

There are more than 100 different types of clouds. The system we currently use to describe clouds was developed about 200 years ago by a British pharmacist named Luke Howard. Evidently, his job didn't take up all of his time, for he devoted tens of thousands of hours to observing what he called the "countenance of the skies." In 1803, Howard published his system of classifying clouds, a system that is so easy to understand, we still use it today.

Howard classified clouds into three basic types according to their shape and height above the ground:

Cirrus (from the Latin word meaning "a lock of hair") are the wispy strands of clouds high in the sky.

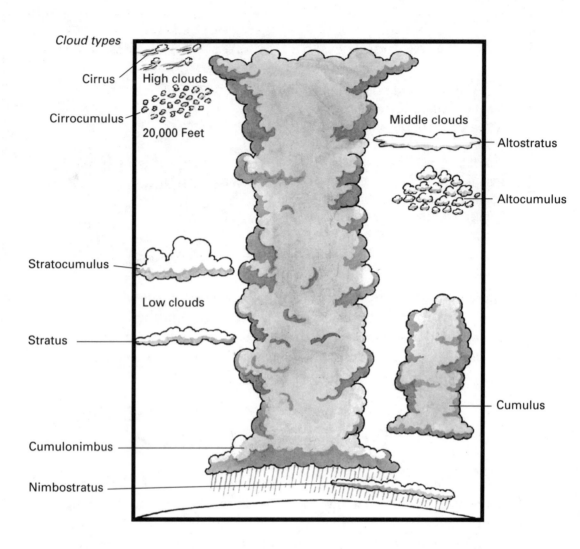

Cloud types

Cirrus · High clouds

Cirrocumulus

20,000 Feet

Middle clouds

Altostratus

Altocumulus

Stratocumulus

Low clouds

Stratus

Cumulus

Cumulonimbus

Nimbostratus

Cumulus (from the Latin word meaning "heap") are the puffy white clouds formed by rising air heated by the sun.

Stratus (from the Latin word meaning "widespread" or layered") are the horizontal blankets of clouds that cover most of the sky.

To describe clouds that produce rain or snow he used the Latin word *nimbus*, which means "cloud," and to separate a higher cloud from a lower cloud of the same type he used the prefix *alto*, which means "high." Finally, Howard combined words to describe a mixture of cloud types, such as *altostratus*, a stratus cloud found high in the sky. *Cumulonimbus*, a very tall cumulus cloud that often brings thunderstorms, is a combination of the Latin words *cumulus*, meaning "heap," and *nimbus*, "cloud." That's a big heap of clouds!

CREATE A CLOUD

A cloud is made of billions of tiny drops of water. Here's how to make your own cloud in a bottle. **You'll need an adult to help you.**

What You Need:
- A clear glass bottle with screw cap
- Plastic drinking straw
- Modeling clay
- Scissors
- Cold water
- Matches

What to Do:
1. First, ask your adult helper to pierce a hole in the bottle cap big enough for the straw to get through with a snug fit.
2. Now take the drinking straw and push it through the hole in the bottle cap.
3. Form the modeling clay around the straw on the top of the cap to seal it.
4. Run the cold water tap in the kitchen until it's very cold. Place the bottle under the tap and pour about one inch of cold water into it. If the tap water isn't very cold, put a cup of water in the refrigerator for a half hour before starting this experiment.
5. Cover the opening of the bottle with your thumb and swish the water around, then pour it out into the sink.
6. Now you're going to fill the bottle with smoke. Ask your adult helper to light the match and blow it out near the neck of the bottle. Quickly place the match inside the neck of the bottle and hold it there until the bottle fills with smoke.
7. Hold your thumb over the top of the bottle so the smoke doesn't escape while you get your bottle cap ready. Quickly put the cap on the bottle and twist it in place.
8. Blow into the straw with four strong, hard breaths.
9. Pinch the straw and set the bottle down.
10. Release the straw and observe!

What Happens and Why:
When you release the straw, the air pressure drops and the air inside cools. This causes the water vapor to condense into tiny droplets that cling to the particles of smoke and form a cloud.

Why Clouds Float Instead of Fall

If you squeeze a spray bottle filled with water, you'll see the mist that comes out slowly drift to the floor or ground. So why doesn't gravity make clouds fall? The reason is that cloud droplets or ice particles are incredibly small and light—it takes 7 billion of them to make up a tablespoon of water! Because they're just a tiny bit heavier than air, they fall very slowly, less than 2 feet per minute, and the slightest puff of wind will send them upward again.

Clouds and Weather Forecasting

Hundreds of years ago, long before the invention of the telephone, radio, or television, some Native American tribes invented a way to talk to each other over long distances. They would build a bonfire, then use a wet blanket to cover and uncover the fire to release different-size puffs of smoke. Other tribe members miles away could read simple messages as the smoke rose into the sky.

Clouds carry messages to us, too, if we learn how to read them. For almost all of human history, people couldn't pick up a newspaper or watch television to find out what the weather

Record Clouds

Tallest: The towering cumulonimbus clouds, or thunderclouds, soar as high as 10 to 11 miles (16–17 km) above Earth.

Rarest: Noctilucent clouds are created in outer space! These faint, fast-moving clouds occur only at altitudes about 50 miles (80 km) over Earth, and they are made of ice-covered dust from broken-up meteors.

Strangest!: Lenticular, or lens-shaped, clouds are formed when air rises to clear a mountain, then is blown downward. Because of their shape and because they tend to give off a strange glow, they are often mistaken for UFOs.

was going to be like. They also had no scientific instruments to rely on. As a result, they spent a lot of time carefully studying the sky. Gradually, they learned that certain types of weather followed the appearance of certain types of clouds, and they used this knowledge to plan their daily activities.

How accurately can you forecast the weather by reading the clouds? Surprising as it may sound, you can predict what the weather will be for the next eight or

Spencer's Cloud Talk

In my weather forecast, here are the terms I use to describe different types of cloud cover:

"Fair" means that less than 40 percent of the sky is covered by clouds.

"Partly sunny" and "partly cloudy" mean that between 30 percent and 70 percent of the sky is covered by clouds. I use "partly sunny" when I think there will be more sun than clouds, and "partly cloudy" when I think there will be more clouds.

"Cloudy" means that more than 70 percent of the sky is covered by clouds.

ten hours nearly as accurately by watching the sky as you can by using all our fancy scientific instruments.

The height of clouds gives a general indication of future weather. The rule is the higher the cloud, the finer the weather. This is true because the more water vapor there is in the air, the more likely it is to rain, and the lower the clouds will hang. Low clouds are heavier than high clouds, contain more moisture, and generally mean that rain or snow is on the way.

Here are some other predictions we can make by looking at clouds:

Cirrus clouds: A few scattered cirrus clouds high in the sky occur in good weather. But when these clouds are connected in long, filmy strands that are sometimes called "mares' tails," they are a very early sign that rain may arrive in the next 24 hours.

Cumulus clouds: The pure-white puffy cumulus clouds that look like cotton balls are signs of good weather. But on hot, humid summer days, watch out when the bottom of cumulus clouds begins to flatten and the cloud begins to grow higher and higher. Towering clouds are formed by the unstable, rising air. This means the cloud is turning into a cumulonimbus cloud that can produce a thunderstorm.

Stratus clouds: Sometimes, on what began as a clear day, stratus clouds move closer and closer together until they cover most of the sky and look like the scales of a fish. This is called a "mackerel sky," and it's a sign of rain. Soon the clouds will form a dark, low stratus cloud, which is almost always a sign that precipitation is going to fall.

Clouds and Earth Temperature

Clouds help control Earth's temperature in two different ways. First, they shade over half the surface of the planet on the average day, making it many degrees cooler. For example, although the tropical areas of our world are always warm, they'd be about 30° hotter if it weren't for the protection of the clouds. Overall, clouds lower the average global temperature by about 15°, which helps keep the ice caps from melting—and flooding the world's coastlines.

At night, clouds act like a blanket, trapping warmer air near the ground. A cloudy winter night can be 10° to 15° warmer than a clear winter night. If there were no clouds to trap heat at all, much of the United States would get too cold at night for crops to grow.

3

Yes, It Really Can Rain Frogs!
RAIN OF ALL SORTS

Just before eight o'clock one Thursday morning in October 1947, a man named A. D. Bajkov and his wife were having breakfast at a restaurant in Marksville, Louisiana, when the waitress came over to their table and made an odd announcement: "**FISH** are falling from the sky!"

Mr. and Mrs. Bajkov rushed outside to see what all the excitement was about. Sure enough, covering the streets, roofs, and yards, and hanging in the trees of the small town were thousands of fresh fish, flapping about in the morning fog.

When we say "It's raining cats and dogs," we don't mean that Garfields and Lassies are falling from the sky—it's just an expression we use to describe heavy rain. But it really did rain fish on that morning in 1947. How could this happen?

Raining Snakes, Frogs, and Fish

No one has ever observed snakes, frogs, fish, or other animals being carried up into the skies. The only logical explanation for these strange rains, however, is that the culprits are **tornadoes,** columns of air that drop down from storm clouds and twirl at very high speed, or **waterspouts,** tornadoes that touch down on water instead of land. There are numerous accounts of tornadoes picking up trucks, automobiles, farm equipment, even entire houses, and depositing them elsewhere.

Large waterspouts have been reported picking up objects as big as a 5-ton houseboat, so it makes sense that they could pick up small creatures like fish and frogs. Once aloft, the living debris could be carried tens, perhaps hundreds, of miles by powerful winds before plummeting to Earth in the downdrafts of a thunderstorm, or dropped when the wind died down.

Some of History's Weirdest, Wackiest, and Totally Bizarre Rains

Eighteen hundred years ago, two towns in Greece experienced a rain of frogs so thick, the ground was completely covered with heaps of the slippery, slimy creatures! Unable to walk the streets or find a water supply that wasn't packed with frogs, most people left town and never came back!

Snails fell with a slow, whirling motion during a light rain shower over Chester, Pennsylvania, in 1869, and a similar report of hundreds of thousands of snails falling from the sky came from Algiers in 1953.

A boy who was walking in the rain in Yuma, Arizona, in 1941 was hit on the shoulder by a falling clam.

Live, dark brown snakes, from 12 to 18 inches long, covered the ground after a torrential rain on Memphis, Tennessee, on December 15, 1876.

Near Dubuque, Iowa, in 1882, a hailstone containing two live frogs fell to the ground. After the ice melted, the frogs hopped away!

There have also been accounts in ancient writings of red, yellow, and milk-white downpours, sometimes described as rains of blood or milk. These rains were probably colored by small particles of dust or plant pollen that had been blown great distances. The Sahara Desert contains areas of reddish iron dust picked up by desert whirlwinds, and in some areas red algae grows so quickly after a storm that it seems as if it fell from the sky. Yellow rains result when certain tree pollens are blown upwards. And gray volcanic ash blown into the sky mixes with water to form a white rain that looks like milk.

Clouds:
The Raw Material of Rain

In chapter 2, we learned the secret of one of nature's magic tricks: water vapor forced upward and cooled condenses around particles of dust to form the droplets that make up clouds. These cloud droplets are the raw material of rain, but they are so tiny that it takes from 1 to 15 million of them to make a single raindrop. Only one out of every ten clouds produces **precipitation,** which is any kind of rain or snow, for two reasons:

- Conditions have to be just right for cloud droplets to make raindrops.
- The air has to contain lots of moisture.

Heavy rain is often caused by the movement of **fronts,** areas where warm air meets cold air. As the warm air rises up over the cool air, it cools down and causes rain. If the warm air becomes partly surrounded by cooler air, the warm air causes an area of lower pressure called a **depression**. A low pressure system moving over us usually brings unsettled and rainy weather. Let's zoom inside a cloud and see precisely how rain is formed.

A warm front meeting a cold front: heavy rain occurs when the warm air rises and cools.

In a depression, cool air surrounds warm air, forming an unsettled area of low pressure.

Presto Changeo—
How Raindrops Are Formed

Super-cooled

The tiny water droplets in clouds don't stick together; they bounce off each other. Scientists were mystified about how raindrops actually formed until they discovered that something very strange happened to those cloud droplets as they were lifted higher above Earth into increasingly cold temperatures. Although water freezes at **32°** Fahrenheit (0° Celsius) on the ground, liquid cloud droplets don't begin to freeze into ice crystals until the temperature drops below 14° Fahrenheit (-9.9° Celsius)—which on a summer day happens 2 to 3 miles above the ground. (**Crystals** are solids made up of molecules that are stuck together in a special way—they are neatly arranged in precise, repeating patterns.) Even more amazingly, some of the water doesn't freeze at all! This "supercooled" water is found at cloud temperatures as low as 10° to 20° *below* zero (-23° to -29° Celsius).

This mixture of ice crystals and supercooled water is the recipe for precipitation. Ice crystals attract water droplets, which join the crystals like tiny ships docking at a space station. The ice crystals gradually get **bigger and bigger** until they are so heavy that they begin to fall. If the temperature below the cloud is above freezing, the crystals melt to form raindrops. If the temperature is below freezing, the crystals will fall to Earth as snow.

Different Kinds of Rain Events

Meteorologists call precipitation a weather "event" (maybe because *anything* having to do with the weather is an event for a meteorologist!). There are three basic kinds of rain events:

- **Drizzle** is like fog that falls to the ground. Drizzle drops are tiny—one-fifth the size of the smallest regular raindrops—and they float downward so slowly that the total precipitation on the ground is too light to measure. Drizzle occurs when a mass of warm, very damp air comes in contact with slightly colder air or colder ground temperatures and forms a low layer of thick, dark clouds.
- **Showers** or **thundershowers** fall in a specific location for a short period of time. In the summer, rain can briefly fall from a cloud directly overhead while

the sun is shining brightly. Showers are caused when an area of damp air is suddenly lifted into the atmosphere by strong air currents to form a rain cloud. The length of the shower is determined by the size of the cloud and the speed at which it's moving. For example, an average-size cloud that produces a shower is 10 miles (16 km) across. If the wind is blowing 20 miles per hour (32 km/hour), it takes 30 minutes for the cloud to pass.

- **Steady rain** that falls for hours generally occurs when a warm front moves over a cold front. The warm, moist air is lighter than the colder air, so it's slowly lifted upwards, producing clouds and rain. If the warm front stalls, or stops moving, rain can fall for days. In the tropical rain forests of South America and Africa, the months of heaviest rainfall are called the rainy season. In the tropics, where the warm air surrounding the equator combines with the moisture from the oceans, there are more than 200 thunderstorms per year.

When Is a Car Like a Weather Forecaster?

Weather reporters describe rain in terms of how much falls in an hour. But the easiest way to classify rain is to watch how your mom, dad, or other drivers use their windshield wipers.

When the wipers are only needed every couple of minutes or so, it means a "trace" of rain or drizzle that's too slight to measure.

Wipers set on intermittent sweep means "light" rain falling at a rate of less than .1 inch (.25 centimeters) per hour.

When the wipers are on constant sweep, it means "moderate" rain falling at a rate of .1 to .3 inches (.25 to .76 centimeters) per hour.

Wipers on high speed indicate "heavy" rain falling at .3 inches (.76 centimeters) or more per hour.

The Whole Dribble on Raindrops

Size   Raindrops vary in size from about 1/110th of an inch (.03 centimeters—smaller than the head of a pin) to just under 1/4 of an inch (.64 centimeters—about the size of a pencil eraser) in **diameter** (the distance through the center from one side to the other). If raindrops get too big, they break in two when they fall.

Shape   Raindrops are often portrayed in a teardrop shape, but they actually look more like **hamburger buns**—flat on the bottom and slightly rounded on top. Air pressure on the falling drop flattens out the bottom.

Speed   The speed of falling raindrops depends on their size and the strength of any air currents or wind. On a calm day, average-size raindrops fall at about 7 miles per hour (11 km/hour), or 600 feet per minute (183 meters/minute). The largest raindrops fall about three times that fast. In strong thunderstorms, however, air currents can propel raindrops to speeds up to 60 or 70 miles per hour (96 to 112 km/hour).

Small raindrops are tiny spheres.

Larger ones, still less than 1/4 of an inch (.64 centimeters) in diameter, bulge out on top and flatten on the bottom.

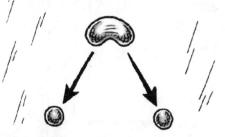

When a drop becomes larger than 1/4 of an inch in diameter, it breaks up into two or more smaller spheres.

MAKE YOUR OWN RAIN GAUGE

Because rain often falls in small amounts, it's easiest to measure when it is collected in a small container. You can make a good, accurate rain gauge with a slender olive bottle.

What You Need:
- A clean, empty olive bottle
- Masking tape
- Ruler
- Pen
- Coffee can

What to Do:
1. Place the ruler inside the coffee can, holding it straight up and down.
2. Pour in 1/2" (1 cm) of water.
3. Fasten a piece of masking tape along the olive bottle from the bottom to the top, cutting it off near the opening of the jar.
4. Pour the water from the coffee can into the olive jar.
5. Mark off 1/4" (.6 cm) on the tape at the water level.
6. Using this 1/4" measurement, continue to mark off 1/4" intervals up to the top of the tape. At the fourth mark, you can also write 1" (2.5 cm).
7. When it rains, place the coffee can outside to collect the rain-water. After the rain stops, pour the water from the coffee can into the small jar and read the measurement.

What Happens and Why:
The rainwater you poured into the small jar represents the amount of rain that has fallen. Meteorologists measure and report rainfall in inches (or centimeters) in the same way–by reading the markings on a rain gauge.

Measuring the Quantity of Rainfall

One thing I like about the weather is that you don't always need a lot of expensive instruments to measure it. For example, you measure rain simply by placing a container outside. The **rain gauge** used at weather stations looks like a coffee can. Rain collects in the top and drains into the container, where it can be measured.

What Is Considered a Lot of Rain?

Any period of rain that measures 1/2 inch or more is considered a heavy rainfall. The wettest region of the United States, the southeastern states, has an average annual rainfall of up to 70 inches (178 cm), or about 6 inches (15 cm) per month. The northeastern and midwestern states have rainfalls ranging from 15 to 50 inches (38 to 127 cm) per year. Among the wettest areas in Europe are the mountains of Scotland, Wales, and northern England, where the rain can fall an average of 200 inches (508 cm) per year.

Wet Extremes

🌍 *Most rained-on place in the world:* Mount Waialeale, Hawaii, with an average 460 inches (11 meters) per year.

🌍 *Biggest holiday splash:* On the Fourth of July in 1956 in Unionville, Maryland, a downpour dropped 1.23 inches (3.08 cm) of rain in one minute!

🌍 *One wet year:* From August 1860 to August 1861, Cherrapunji, India, received 1,042 inches (26.5 meters) of rain.

What Is Acid Rain?

Cloud droplets form around any tiny particles floating in the air—even ones that shouldn't be there. Among the most dangerous are bits of sulfur and nitric oxides released through the smokestacks of factories and power plants. When these oxides combine with water, they form sulfuric and nitric acids, which fall with rain.

Because the particles can be carried thousands of miles by upper-level winds (just like snakes and frogs!), acid rain is a problem in many areas of the world. In Canada, the northern United States, and northern Europe, acid rain has defoliated trees, damaged plant life, and killed plants and fish in lakes and streams. Acid rain also eats away at buildings and other structures—including Egypt's famous Sphinx.

Trying to Control the Weather: Making Rain

We know from archaeological finds that people have been searching for a way to make it rain for at least 5,000 years, primarily through dances and other rituals. Rain dancers are depicted in Egyptian tomb paintings dating back to 3,000 B.C. Native American tribes used a wide variety of items ranging from snakes to special face paints to jugs of water. In southeastern Europe, young girls went from house to house to get water poured on them, and as recently as 1992, riots broke out in Somalia because people believed that a long dry spell was caused by women wearing skirts that were too short.

Unfortunately, there is no scientific proof that any of these dances or rituals actually work. Equally unfortunately, modern science has been unable to provide any long-term solution to the problems of people living in areas suffering serious **droughts** (long periods with little or no rainfall). Rain requires a stream of moist air blowing overland from the ocean; until we learn how to change the direction of the wind (an unlikely prospect), drought relief can come only when weather patterns change.

However, in the past half century scientists have made some discoveries about how to get more moisture out of clouds. This process is called **cloud seeding**.

What Is Cloud Seeding?

The first scientific breakthrough in rainmaking came in 1946. For months, a scientist named Vincent J. Schaefer had been trying to make artificial clouds in a box by placing numerous substances from volcanic ash to talcum powder into it. Then one day, Schaefer discovered his "cold box" had gotten too warm, so he tossed in a block of dry ice, which is carbon dioxide gas

Shoppers' Alert: Snowstorm in Aisle 4!

One day, while experimenting with silver iodide, physicist Bernard Vonnegut whipped up a batch of the chemical in a smoke generator. The smoke drifted out of his lab, cruised on the breeze for about 6 miles (10 km), entered a grocery store, and started a small snowstorm in the frozen-food section!

Silver oxide works best at getting additional moisture out of clouds that are already producing some precipitation. In forming rain in the first place, nature is still far more effective than any advanced scientific techniques created by people.

FROZEN FOOD

turned to solid by lowering the temperature to −108° Fahrenheit (−77° Celsius). To the astonishment of the scientist, something strange and wonderful happened— the dry ice caused a tiny blue cloud of ice crystals to form.

Rainmaker or Clever Con Man?

The "science" of rainmaking had become a very controversial topic in the United States by the time Charles Mallory Hatfield came on the scene early in the twentieth century. The most famous of all "rainmakers," Hatfield had a secret chemical formula that worked many times, but was harshly criticized by professional meteorologists.

On January 13, 1916 (a Friday!), Hatfield and his brother began their most talked-about rainmaking event ever. They promised they could provide enough rain to fill up San Diego's Morena Reservoir, which was dangerously low due to drought. Perched on a 20-foot-high tower near Morena Dam, Hatfield built a fire and began burning his concoction, sending its **foul-smelling** fumes into the sky. The next day, around noon, it started to rain. And it kept raining. The downpour lasted for days, causing disastrous floods, and did not end until January 29. But Hatfield was successful: the reservoir was filled to within 5 inches of the top.

There is no proof that Hatfield's secret formula was responsible for the rain. Some scientists believe that rainmakers appear to be successful because they're experts at reading the signs, and know when rain is coming. In other words, rainmakers like Hatfield were either the pioneers of cloud seeding or some of the most sensational con men the country has ever seen!

Schaefer soon discovered that he could use dry ice to create miniature snow-storms in his little box. On November 13 of that same year, he put his discovery to the test by releasing dry ice into a 14,000-foot-high cloud over Mount Greylock in Massachusetts. Moments later, snowflakes formed that fell 2,000 feet before evaporating.

Using dry ice in large quantities proved to be impractical. But scientists soon discovered that a substance called silver iodide worked even better. The microscopic structure of silver iodide crystals is virtually identical to that of ice crystals. So when they enter a cloud, they attract supercooled water drops just as ice crystals do, and the drops then get heavy enough to fall as rain. The crystals are either dropped from an airplane or burned with other substances that carry them upward in smoke.

Scientists' attempts to change the weather are called **weather modification**. Putting silver iodide into a cloud to make it gain more moisture is called cloud seeding. Although controversial, it is taken very seriously in places where crops grow. North Dakota, for example, spends over a million dollars every year seeding clouds so that farmers will have a few more inches of rain during the growing season.

Nature's Sound and Light Shows

THUNDER AND LIGHTNING

Thunderstorms can produce strong feelings of anxiety and just plain fear in people of all ages. That's why ancient peoples believed that thunder and lightning were the weapons of **angry gods**.

Today, we know that gods don't hurl bolts of lightning. However, the facts about thunderstorms are more amazing than the myths. Thunderstorms are by far the most common weather event, occurring 16 million times per year. At any given moment, an average of 1,800 thunderstorms are raging somewhere.

The average thunderstorm drops *1 billion pounds* (454,000,000 kilograms) of water in 15 to 25 minutes while producing lightning bolts that each contain enough power to light 200,000 homes!

An Electrifying Experience

I witnessed many severe thunderstorms, or electrical storms as we called them, while I was growing up in Virginia. A couple of times I even saw lightning strike a tree with a blast that sounded like a bomb going off, splitting the tree in half. But one storm that my little brother and I will never forget is the one that carried lightning right into our house!

During this severe thunderstorm, my mother walked over to unplug an electric clock that was on a table in front of a window in the living room. As her hand reached toward the clock, lightning struck nearby and something that looked like a ball of fire came right through the window, through the clock, and struck her on the arm. She was knocked to the floor by the power of the electric charge, and her arm was paralyzed for a few seconds. She wasn't seriously hurt, and felt okay in a few minutes. But that's not the end of the story.

About five minutes later, my father went to lock the back door, which was rattling in the wind. As he reached for the metal door handle, the same thing happened to him—a ball of fire popped out of the doorknob, went up his arm and into the middle of his body. He told us that he felt like someone had punched him in the stomach! Neither of my parents were seriously hurt, thank goodness, and they didn't even have to go to the hospital. But this storm taught me to respect the awesome forces of electricity in every thunderstorm—and to be even more curious about nature's amazing sound and light shows.

What Is a Thunderstorm?

Producing thunder and lightning requires an enormous amount of energy. As you read in chapter 2, this energy is built up in a special kind of a cloud called a cumulonimbus cloud.

Cumulonimbus (thunderclouds) are huge, towering, mountainous masses that can reach heights of 60,000 feet (18,288 meters). Thunderclouds require more moisture and more heat than other clouds, which is why they are most common in warmer weather.

There are three basic conditions that produce thunderstorms:

- **Air mass thunderclouds** are common late afternoon occurrences in very hot, sticky weather. Warm air near the ground is trapped by a blanket of cooler air above. Intense sunshine heats the air all day, building up pressure until it finally "boils," breaking through the blanket of cool air to form the cloud mass that produces thunder and lightning.

- **Mountain thunderstorms** form on hot, sticky days in mountainous regions because the air around elevated peaks is colder than the air over valley areas. Afternoon breezes that flow up the sides of mountains produce the updrafts that cause thunderclouds to form.
- **Frontal thunderclouds** produce by far the most violent storms. They occur when a mass of cold air collides with a mass of very warm, moist air. Because the cold air is heavier than warm, moist air, it acts like a wedge, driving underneath the warm air and lifting it upward with great force. Frontal thunderstorms often produce high winds, hail, and tornadoes.

No Place for a Picnic

Bogor, in Indonesia, experiences the most thunderstorms of any city on Earth, with 322 thunderstorm-days per year.

In a thunderstorm, warm air rises and cool air drops toward Earth with precipitation.

What Happens Inside a Thunderstorm?

The action begins when warm air boils upward until it becomes cool enough to condense into water droplets. This condensation releases heat, which pushes the water droplets higher and higher until they form ice crystals. In many thunderstorms, the energy is so great that the ice crystals are pushed to the very top of the lower layer of the atmosphere, 12 miles (19 km) above the ground. Because of the great height, the crystals tend to be larger and produce larger raindrops.

Finally, the force of gravity takes over and the ice crystals fall, melting on the way down to produce heavy rains. At its peak, a thunderstorm is like a two-lane highway, with updrafts feeding warm, moist air into the storm and a downdraft of cooled air and precipitation falling. Eventually, the downdrafts choke off the updrafts. With no new moist air as fuel, the thunderstorm ends and the thundercloud breaks up.

What Causes Lightning?

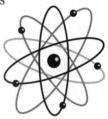

Scientists do not yet fully understand what causes lightning. Clouds are made up of **atoms**, the smallest units of matter. Atoms contain **electrons**, which have a negative electrical charge. In a thundercloud, some atoms lose electrons and some atoms pick up extra electrons. Scientists think that the cloud's atoms crash into each other in the high winds of a thunderstorm, and lose or gain electrons when they collide. Atoms that lose electrons have a *positive* charge, and atoms that gain electrons have a *negative* charge. A charged atom is called an **ion**. Just like in a pair of magnets, opposite charges attract each other and the same charges resist each other.

Intracloud lightning

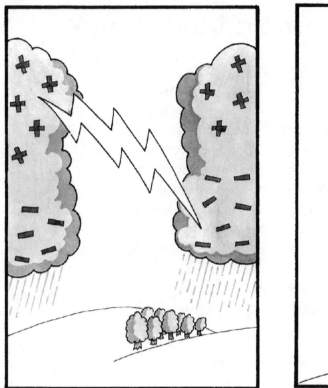

Cloud-to-cloud lightning

Cloud-to-ground lightning

n the thundercloud, the positive ions cluster together at the top of the cloud and the negative ones at the bottom. When these clusters grow, they increase in charge. This makes the attraction between the upper and lower parts of the cloud stronger and stronger. The strong electrical attraction between the positive and negative charges makes a lightning bolt leap between the two areas. Lightning is a giant spark.

Earth also contains ions. As the stormcloud passes over, the negative charge at the bottom of the cloud makes something happen to the ions on Earth's surface. Positive charges are attracted by the negative charges passing overhead. The charge from the ground is being pulled toward the opposite charge at the bottom of the cloud. What happens when the attraction gets very strong? Lightning leaps between the gap from the cloud to Earth!

Lightning can flash in three ways: within a cloud **(intracloud lightning)**, from one cloud to another **(cloud-to-cloud lightning)**, and from the cloud to the ground **(cloud-to-ground lightning)**. On the average, 80 percent of lightning bolts are intracloud or cloud-to-cloud, and 20 percent are cloud-to-ground.

Cloud-to-ground lightning tries to find the shortest path between a cloud and the ground. This means it will be led to the tallest nearby object—and that's why it's **dangerous** to be standing out in the open, or near a tree, during a thunderstorm.

A Journey Inside a Flash of Lightning

Let's start with a surprising fact: the flash of lightning you see is not caused by negative ions moving towards the ground. The stream of ions, which is only a few inches wide, is invisible, and is called a **leader**. When this stream nears the ground, however, it draws a stream of positive ions towards it—normally through something tall, like a tree or lightning rod. When the two streams meet, they form a pencil-thin path for electric current to flow from ground to cloud.

This flow, called the **return stroke,** produces the intensely brilliant flash that we call lightning. The ions in the electric current are moving so fast that they cause the air around them to **glow**, creating the light you see in lightning. The electric current travels at 60,000 miles per second (96,558 km/second), about one-third the speed of light, which means that each stroke lasts about .02 of a second. That's fast enough to travel around the world in one second! Lightning seems to flicker because what we see as a single lightning bolt actually consists of an average of forty-two separate return strokes that combined take less than one second.

A lightning bolt consists of the leader coming down to the ground and the return stroke rising up from Earth.

Lightning by Any Other Name . . .

There are several different terms used to describe lightning:

- "Streak" lightning is the ordinary zigzag bolt from cloud to ground.
    - "Heat" lightning is streak lightning that's so far away that thunder can't be heard.
    - "Fork" lightning is a bolt that seems to break into several fingers that hit the ground at the same time.
- "Ribbon" lightning is streak lightning that looks filmy because the channel is blown sideways by strong winds.
- "Sheet" lightning is a white glow caused by the diffusion of many lightning strokes in distant clouds.
- "Ball" lightning is a very rare phenomenon in which a pear-shaped ball of reddish or whitish light floats horizontally before exploding. Scientists can't explain why this occurs.

What Causes Thunder?

One ancient theory for the cause of **thunder** came from the Roman philosopher Lucretius, who thought it was the result of clouds crashing into each other. It's a pretty good theory for someone living between 100-55 B.C., a time when a lot of people thought that thunderbolts were zaps from the god Jupiter. But we now know that thunder is caused by lightning. A lightning bolt heats the air through which it passes to an astounding 50,000° Fahrenheit, almost five times the temperature of the surface of the sun. The heat causes the air to expand with an explosive force that produces a loud sound. In other words, what we call thunder are the sound waves that blast out from superheated air around a lightning bolt.

How Far Away Is That Lightning Bolt?

Thunder and lightning occur at the same time, but light, which travels at a speed of 186,000 miles per second, reaches your eye almost instantaneously. Thunder, however, travels at a pokey 1,100 feet per second, the speed of sound. To get a rough idea of the distance between you and a lightning strike, count the seconds ("one, one thousand . . . two, one thousand . . . ") between the time you see the flash and the time you hear the thunder. Every 5 seconds you count is a distance of about 1.2 miles (about 2 km). If the storm is traveling away from you, the length of time between a flash and the sound of the thunder will become longer and longer. If it is coming toward you, the time will become shorter and shorter.

The word "Thursday" comes from "Thor's Day," named for the thunder god of Norse (Scandinavian) mythology.

You'll know when the storm is right on top of you if you can't even count to one before you hear the thunder!

You can also the tell the difference between thunder that is close and thunder that is far away from just the sound itself. Thunder is produced by a series of **explosions**. If you're close to the lightning strike, the sound of the explosions blends together into one, sharp crack. However, if you are farther

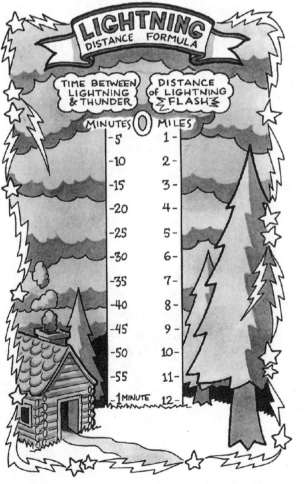

The lightning distance formula

away, the sound separates into a longer rumble. The farthest away you can hear thunder is about 15 to 18 miles (24 to 29 km).

How Dangerous Is Lightning?

🌍 Lightning kills about 100 people per year, or about 1 out of every 500,000 people.

🌍 Another 500 people are injured by lightning every year.

🌍 Lightning courses through a body at speeds of 90,000 miles (145,000 km) per second—so fast that it often doesn't leave permanent injury.

🌍 Lightning causes about 40 percent of all farm fires and about 10 to 15 percent of all forest fires each year.

How to Protect Yourself from Lightning

🌍 Seek cover when the sky begins to darken with thick clouds.

🌍 If you are stuck outside, never take cover under a tree; instead, lie flat on any spot lower than the rest of the ground around it.

🌍 Don't ride a bike, push a lawn mower, ride a tractor, pick up a rake, golf club, or any other metal tool or toy during a thunderstorm.

🌍 If you're in a car or other vehicle, stay there. You're only in danger when you're outside, touching the car and the ground at the same time.

🌍 Inside, don't use the phone, take a shower, or hold an electrical appliance.

LET'S MAKE SOME STATIC

In this activity, we'll create an electrical charge called static electricity. This is like the electrical charge created in a thundercloud, but much weaker and not at all dangerous. On a small scale, you can make atoms crash together and become ions—not by using violent winds like those in a thundercloud—but by rubbing two things together.

What You Need:
- A comb

- A wool sweater, scarf, or other wool object

- A piece of scrap paper

What to Do:
1. Tear the paper into tiny pieces.
2. Rub the comb hard across the wool several times.
3. Touch the comb to the bits of paper.
4. Rub the comb again, then touch it. Do you feel anything?

What Happens and Why:
The bits of paper cling to the comb. By rubbing the comb against the wool, you make the atoms on the surface of the comb collide and become ions. The ions in the comb attract the atoms in the paper, and draw the paper toward the comb. When you touch the comb, you may get a tiny shock. This is a miniversion of a lightning bolt leaping between two areas that have opposite charges, like the bottom of a stormcloud and the ground. But a lightning bolt is many billions of times stronger than the electricity you create between the comb and the paper.

About Ben Franklin and That Kite

As my family learned from the thunderstorm I told you about at the beginning of this chapter, lightning can travel into a house or other building. The electricity that strikes a building can travel through the telephone wires, plumbing system, or electrical wire. But thanks to all-around total genius Benjamin Franklin, there's a good way to safeguard against it—the lightning rod.

In his famous experiment of 1752, Ben Franklin flew a kite high into the air during a thunderstorm and hung a **key** from the wet kite string. An electrical charge traveled down the string, and when Ben touched the key with his knuckle it made a spark. This proved to him that lightning is a kind of electricity.

Being the brilliant and practical guy that he was, Ben put this discovery to good use by creating an invention that would protect his house in Philadelphia, and the houses of some of his friends, from lightning.

As we just learned, lightning always looks for the highest point on the ground. Lightning will be led to a lightning rod on the top of a house or building. Attached to the rod is a wire that leads the charge harmlessly to the ground, and prevents it from entering the electrical system or other parts of the house. The interior of a large building like a skyscraper is protected by the big steel framework that supports the building. Lightning travels down the metal into the ground, bypassing the electrical systems inside the building.

One Last Crack at the Thunderstorm

We've learned that there are always thunderstorms occurring somewhere over Earth, and that the most common ones blow over in about 15 minutes. But there is one type of thunderstorm that doesn't blow over quickly. **Supercell thunderstorms** are the most powerful and longest-lasting thunderstorms. In the United States, they occur most often in April, May, and June, when the temperature contrast between cold air coming down from Canada and warm, humid air coming north from the Gulf of Mexico is very large. When the two air masses slam into each other, the force of the air moving upward causes the air to begin to spin, forming what is called a **mesocyclone**.

An Old Saying That *Isn't* True

"Lightning never strikes twice in the same place."

Wrong!

Lightning not only can strike twice, it often does. For example, the top of the Empire State Building has been struck a dozen times in a single storm and as often as 500 times per year.

The energy of the spinning draws in more and more air, producing clouds that can range from 10 miles to 250 miles (16 to 400 kilometers) in diameter.

Supercell thunderstorms can last several hours, and because the air is already spinning, they are likely to cause tornadoes.

5

Wild Winds

THE AWESOME POWER OF HURRICANES AND TORNADOES

Every year, powerful and deadly creatures emerge from the oceans. They come from the Atlantic, the Pacific, the Indian Ocean. They're hurricanes, gigantic tropical storms that, near the center or "eye," can have the force equal to an **atomic bomb!** With wind speeds ranging from 75 to 220 miles per hour (120 to 354 km/hour), hurricanes can cover a path 200 to 600 miles (322 to 965 km) wide and travel thousands of miles. They bring power outages, flooding, tree damage, and other destruction to tens of millions of people.

But amazingly, another weather event has winds two to three times those found in the center of hurricanes. Tornadoes can pick up railroad cars, tractor-trailer trucks, even entire buildings, and carry them as far as a half mile. Although these powerful storms may last only for minutes and follow paths as narrow as 50 yards (46 meters), their winds—which can reach 300 miles per hour (483 km/hour)—are often deadly.

What Is a Hurricane?

A hurricane is the most severe kind of tropical **cyclone**. A cyclone is a storm with winds that spin around a low pressure system. In the northern hemisphere, where we live, these winds spin in a counterclockwise direction.

Hurricanes are called tropical storms because they all start in tropical waters, even though they may travel to much colder areas. We label tropical cyclones according to the sustained speed of the winds near the center of the storm:

- A **tropical depression** has winds of 38 miles per hour (61 km/hour) or less
- A **tropical storm** has winds of 39 to 74 miles per hour (62 to 119 km/hour)
- A **hurricane** has winds of 75 miles per hour (120 km/hour) or more

Where in the World Do Hurricanes Form?

If you want to boil water, you put the kettle on the stove and turn on the heat. If you want to cook up a severe storm, you also need heat—in this case, ocean waters with a temperature of 80 ° Fahrenheit (26° Celsius) or warmer, which are only found in the tropics. Above about 30 ° north latitude, water temperatures are too cold.

Tropical cyclones occur all around the Earth. But the only storms that reach the mainland of the United States are those that form in the Atlantic Ocean. That's because the prevailing winds in the latitudes at which hurricanes form always blow from east to west. (See chapter 1 for more on prevailing winds.) That means:

- Hurricanes that form in the Atlantic Ocean are blown toward North America.
- Hurricanes that form in the Pacific Ocean are called typhoons and blow toward Asia.

Hurricane Hazel

When I was seven years old, late in the summer Hurricane Hazel ripped right through our little town—and right over our house. The wind was blowing more than 100 miles per hour, and from our safe spot beneath the kitchen table, my brother and I could hear the frightening howl of the wind and creaking of the trees. When we dared to peek out from under the table to look out the window, we were in for the sight of our lives! Cats and dogs were flying through the air, as well as lawn furniture and trees!

Suddenly the storm was over, or so we thought. But our mother told us that the eerie calm meant that the eye of the storm was passing over, and that it would all start up again soon. She was right! After a few minutes, the wind came back in all its fury. It took our little town quite a while to recover from this hurricane, and we went without power for about two weeks. Even more frightening than lightning and thunder, Hurricane Hazel increased my respect for the forces of nature and made me even more fascinated with weather and science.

When Is Hurricane Season?

Hurricanes don't form in the winter and spring because the ocean waters are too cold. Hurricane season officially begins June 1, but the most severe storms usually occur in August and September, when the ocean temperatures are at their warmest. The water temperatures (and the chances of severe storms) then gradually lower until the official end of hurricane season on November 30.

About five hurricanes strike the United States coastline every 3 years. Of these five, two are likely to be major hurricanes (category 3 or greater on the Saffir-Simpson Hurricane Scale).

What Is the Structure of a Hurricane?

The nickname for hurricanes—"one-eyed monsters"—explains why they are the easiest weather systems to spot on a satellite photo. A typical hurricane measures about 1,000 miles (1,600 kilometers) across, and is formed of a swirling collection of huge cumulus and cumulonimbus storm clouds. The mass of clouds spins counterclockwise around a small clear spot that's called the hurricane eye.

Inside the Eye of the Storm

At the center of a hurricane is an area of pressure so low that air is sucked directly downward and warmed. This downward movement dries up the air and produces a calm, clear area 7 to 20 miles (11–32 km) across. However, the band of clouds surrounding the eye, which is called the **eye wall,** contains the strongest of a hurricane's winds.

The eye produces a strange effect on anyone in the direct path of a hurricane. One moment, the hurricane's violence has escalated to torrential rains and wind gusts of 100 miles per hour (160 km/hour) or more. The next moment, the rain ends, the wind stops, and the sun comes out. For a little while, it seems as if the storm has ended. Then, just as suddenly, the sun fades and the intense pounding begins anew. Ships at sea have survived hurricanes by staying within the eye and sailing at the same speed as the storm.

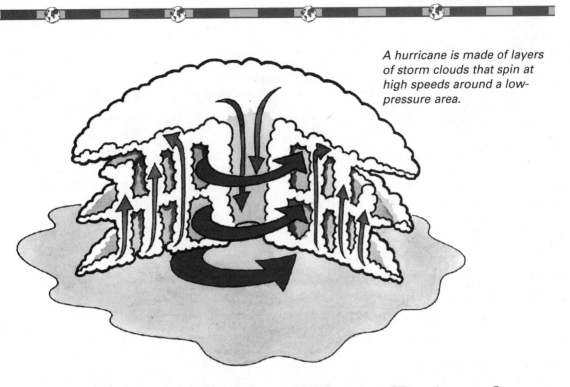

A hurricane is made of layers of storm clouds that spin at high speeds around a low-pressure area.

How Do We Track and Measure Hurricanes?

The National Hurricane Center in Coral Gables, Florida, has the job of monitoring hurricanes. Experts there watch the storms develop using satellite photographs and sophisticated radar. Then, when the hurricanes approach the Caribbean Sea and the U.S. mainland, courageous pilots and crews fly airplanes directly into the storms to measure their exact locations, size, and wind speed. These aircraft, called WP-3s, actually flying laboratories, are among the world's most heavily equipped research aircraft. By flying into the eye of a hurricane, the crew can transmit important storm data to the National Hurricane Center through direct satellite communications. This information is vital to making predictions and warnings about hurricanes.

The crew learns the strength and destructive potential of the storm by measuring the air pressure in the eye of the hurricane. The lower the air pressure, the stronger the storm. They also measure the wind speed within the hurricane, and the speed at which the hurricane is moving across the ocean. Another important measurement is the height of **storm surge**. This is the giant wave that surrounds the hurricane. The force of the hurricane winds blows the ocean up into a wall of water that can be 20 feet (6 meters) high by the time it hits land. When the storm surge crashes over land, it can destroy everything in its path.

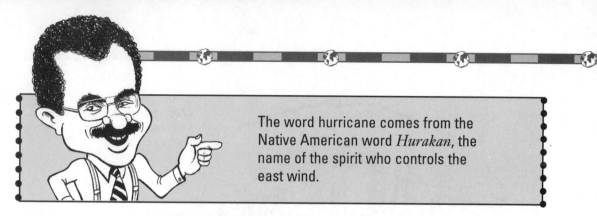

The word hurricane comes from the Native American word *Hurakan*, the name of the spirit who controls the east wind.

Each of these measurements allows forecasters to predict when a hurricane may reach land and how powerful it will be.

Rating the Strength of Hurricanes

Hurricanes are rated in strength from 1 to 5 on the Saffir-Simpson Hurricane Scale:

Scale	Wind Speed Miles per Hour		Storm Surge	Damage
1	74–95	(119–153 km/hour)	4–5 feet (1.2–1.5 m)	Minimal
2	96–110	(154–177 km/hour)	6–8 feet (1.8–2.4 m)	Moderate
3	111–130	(178–209 km/hour)	9–12 feet (3–3.6 m)	Extensive
4	131–155	(210–249 km/hour)	13–18 feet (4–5.5 m)	Extreme
5	More than 155	(more than 249 km/hour)	More than 18 feet (5.5m)	Catastrophic

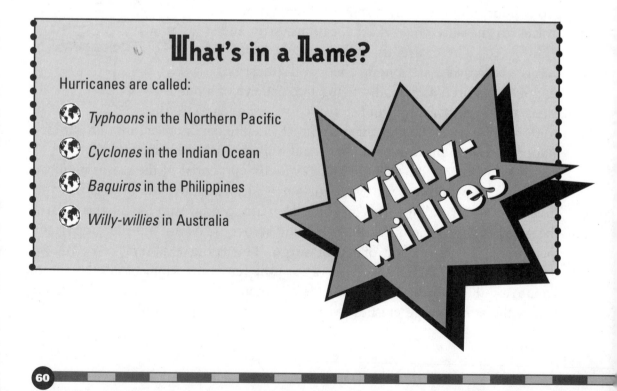

What's in a Name?

Hurricanes are called:

- *Typhoons* in the Northern Pacific
- *Cyclones* in the Indian Ocean
- *Baquiros* in the Philippines
- *Willy-willies* in Australia

Willy-willies

A Storm by Any Other Name . . .

For hundreds of years, hurricanes that formed in the West Indies were named after the saint's day on which they occurred. (A Catholic calendar gives a saint's name to every day of the year.)

During World War II, the practice of giving women's names to hurricanes became popular. Meteorologists in the U.S. military named storms after their wives and girlfriends. The idea caught on, and in 1953 the National Weather Service officially began naming hurricanes with women's names. For over twenty years, hurricanes were given names such as Carla, Donna, Camille, and Agnes.

But all this changed in 1978, when men's *and* women's names were included in storm lists. The list officially used by the World Meteorological Organization contains short, easy-to-remember male and female names from three languages: English, French, and Spanish. The lists repeat themselves every six years, but names that have been given to especially destructive storms are removed and never used again.

What Makes a Hurricane Move Along Its Route?

Hurricanes are pushed along by the prevailing winds. This means their usual path is to move west with the trade winds until they reach about 30 degrees north latitude (about as far north as Jacksonville, Florida). Then they're pushed northeast by the mid-latitude winds. Another factor in the movement of hurricanes is the jet stream. If that powerful wind forms a trough, dipping southward before looping back north, it can steer a hurricane into the Middle Atlantic or New England states.

However, meteorologists don't completely understand why hurricanes travel and behave the way they do. Tracking them with satellite photos has made it much easier to predict which ones may hit land, but this technology hasn't solved every hurricane mystery. Why do they suddenly change direction—a little or a lot—as they roll along with a prevailing wind? Why do they sometimes die when the water is warm and the storm is really cooking? Hurricanes often act in unpredictable ways. But there are two conditions that will always slow a hurricane down for good. Hurricanes get their energy from warm water. They die when that supply of water is cut off because the hurricane strikes land or moves over colder water.

The World's Worst Hurricanes

The most powerful hurricane of the twentieth century was Hurricane Gilbert, which ravaged the Caribbean and the Gulf of Mexico with winds as high as 218 miles per hour (350 km/hour) in 1988. The most powerful storms to hit the United States were Hurricane Camille, which devastated Mississippi in 1969, and an unnamed hurricane that killed 2,000 people in the Florida Keys in 1935. The third most powerful storm, 1992's Hurricane Andrew, set a dubious record by causing $12 billion in damage when it smashed first into southern Florida, then into Louisiana.

However, by far the most deadly storm was a hurricane that hit Galveston, Texas, in June 1900. (I wasn't around yet to report on that one.) Without radar, satellites, or other warning systems, the residents of the low-lying city right on the coast of the Gulf of Mexico were trapped when the violent storm suddenly appeared and destroyed the only bridge to high ground. More than 6,000 people died and the city was totally leveled by the wind and rain.

Weather reporting has taken me to several hurricane sites. I'll never forget driving through Hurricane Opal in October 1995, as it moved through Alabama. I was driving from Atlanta, Georgia—the nearest airport that was open due to the storm—to Mobile, Alabama, to do a broadcast. It was very dark in the early afternoon, with heavy stormclouds filling the sky. Three hours into the drive I hit the most intense part of the storm, with winds blowing at 95 miles per hour (152 km/hour). There was so much rain that I could only see about 10 feet (3 meters) in any direction. The fierce winds blew down power lines and trees along the road. I managed to drive around the flooded parts of the road, even though some cars were stalling in the rising water. And somehow I kept the car steady, hanging on to the steering wheel for dear life! This drive gave me a firsthand experience of hurricane winds and the power of nature at her wildest and most destructive.

What Is a Tornado?

A **tornado**, also called a twister, is a violently rotating column of air extending from a thunderstorm to the ground. The damage from tornadoes comes from the high winds and flying objects it throws around at speeds of 250 miles per hour (400 km/hour) or more. The tornado's path of destruction can be more than 1 mile (1.6 km) wide and 50 miles (80 km) long. Once a tornado in Broken Bow, Oklahoma, carried a motel sign 30 miles (48 km) and dropped it in Arkansas!

What Makes a Twister Twist?

 Although meteorologists are still trying to figure out exactly how tornadoes form, they do know that virtually all tornadoes are born in thunderclouds when the air temperature is at least 65° Fahrenheit (18° Celsius). As we've learned, thunderstorms occur when warm, moist air suddenly begins to rise. Sometimes, upper level wind currents cause warm and cold air to mix and begin to spin. The huge, spinning mass of air is called a mesocyclone. A tornado is a funnel that drops from the bottom of the meso-cyclone. Tornadoes tend to appear after the heaviest rains of a thunderstorm have already fallen. This fact leads meteorologists to believe that the downward air currents produced by the rain guide the funnel cloud to the ground.

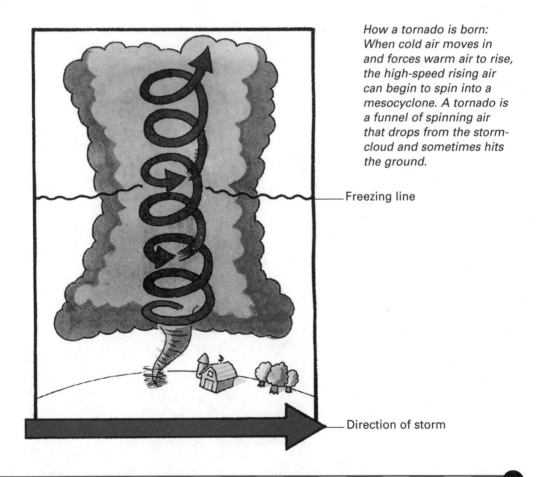

How a tornado is born: When cold air moves in and forces warm air to rise, the high-speed rising air can begin to spin into a mesocyclone. A tornado is a funnel of spinning air that drops from the storm-cloud and sometimes hits the ground.

Freezing line

Direction of storm

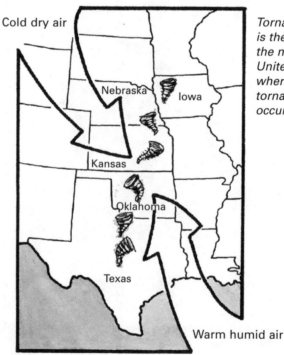

Nowhere on Earth are the winds faster than in a severe tornado. Moderate winds that are sucked into the spinning core, or **vortex** of the storm, revolve faster and faster as they near the center. You've seen this principle in action if you've seen a figure skater perform a spin—the skater twirls faster when she pulls in her arms and legs.

Tornadoes can be produced by any thunderstorm, including the bands of thunderstorms inside hurricanes. Hurricane Gilbert caused some thirty-nine tornadoes in Texas! However, the most intense and deadly tornadoes are spawned by the most violent thunderstorms that occur when very warm and very cold air masses come into contact.

Where Do Most Tornadoes Happen?

Relatively flat land and specific wind patterns make the central United States the world's capital of thunderstorms and tornadoes. With no mountains to run into and slow them down, the cold Arctic air that blows down from the north and the warm, moist air coming up from the Gulf of Mexico and the Caribbean Sea hit each other head-on. The core of this tornado-prone area is called Tornado Alley.

In contrast, mountain ranges in Europe and Asia generally keep very cold and very warm air masses apart. This accident of geography means that the United States has by far the most violent thunderstorms along with the tornadoes they spawn.

Although the greatest number of tornadoes occur in the United States, they also develop with thunderstorms in other places throughout the world, including Australia, Great Britain, China, France, Germany, Hungary, India, Japan, and the Commonwealth of Independent States (the former Soviet Union). Tornadoes can also accompany tropical storms and hurricanes that move over the land in the tropics.

Cold dry air

Nebraska   Iowa

Kansas

Oklahoma

Texas

Warm humid air

Tornado Alley is the area in the midwestern United States where most tornadoes occur.

Tornado Weirdness

Tornadoes have been reported to do strange things, such as:

 Pluck the feathers from chickens

 Drive wooden planks through steel

 Shear the wool off sheep

 Suck soda from open bottles

 Tattoo people for life by driving sand and grit deep beneath their skin

 Lift sleeping babies from their cradles, carry them through the air, and place them safely down—still asleep—hundreds of feet away

Only about **1** thunderstorm in every **1,000** produces a tornado.

The Power of Tornado Winds

No wind-measuring instrument has ever survived a direct encounter with a tornado. So we have to make do with other methods that estimate wind strength, such as radar that tracks the speed of particles caught up in the tornado. By these estimates, we know that winds inside a tornado can exceed 300 miles per hour.

The level of damage those winds can cause is incredible. While hurricanes bend and break trees, tornadoes can uproot trees from the ground and send them hurtling through the air like giant arrows. And, like hurricanes, tornadoes can pick up animals, too. We've already read about waterspouts, which form over water and can pick up fish and frogs. When they touch or get very

Tornadoes Come in Many Shapes and Sizes

There are three general types of tornadoes:

Weak Tornadoes

 Winds less than 100 mph (160 km/hour)

 Lasts 1 to 10 minutes

69 percent of all tornadoes

Less than 5 percent of tornado deaths

Strong Tornadoes

 Winds of 110 to 205 mph (177–329 km/hour)

 Can last 20 minutes or longer

29 percent of all tornadoes

Nearly 30 percent of tornado deaths

Violent Tornadoes

 Winds greater than 205 mph (329 km/hour)

 Can last more than 1 hour

 Only 2 percent of all tornadoes

70 percent of tornado deaths

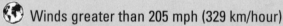

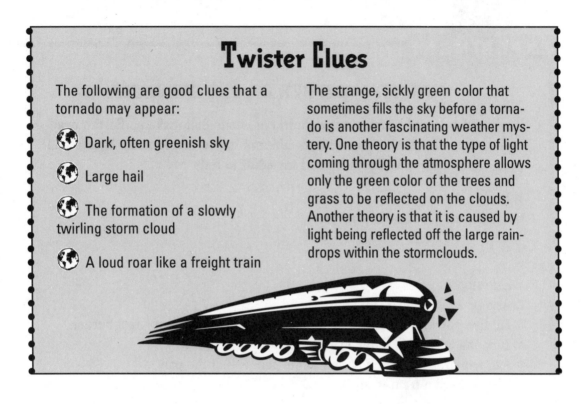

Twister Clues

The following are good clues that a tornado may appear:

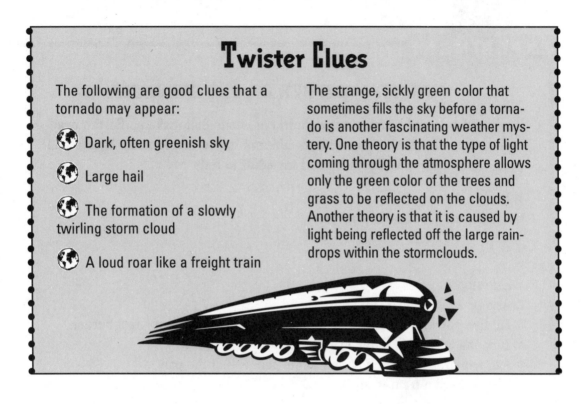 Dark, often greenish sky

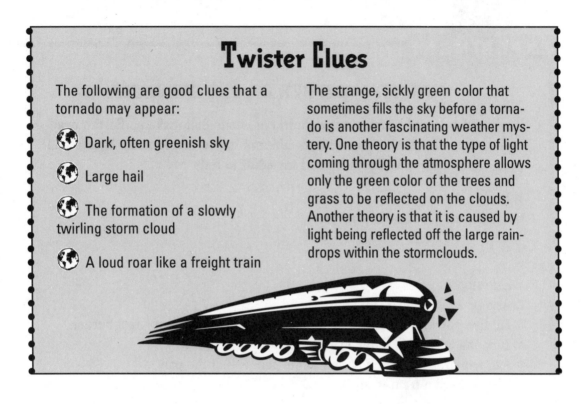 Large hail

 The formation of a slowly twirling storm cloud

 A loud roar like a freight train

The strange, sickly green color that sometimes fills the sky before a tornado is another fascinating weather mystery. One theory is that the type of light coming through the atmosphere allows only the green color of the trees and grass to be reflected on the clouds. Another theory is that it is caused by light being reflected off the large raindrops within the stormclouds.

close to the ground tornadoes can pick up animals—animals as big as cattle. Tornadoes have carried automobiles, trucks, even railroad cars distances of several hundred yards.

Some tornadoes are made up of a cluster of five or six smaller twisters inside the main funnel. These straying arms cause the bizarre patterns of damage that leave survivors scratching their heads, such as when one house is completely destroyed and the house across the street is untouched.

What Is the Life Span of a Tornado?

A funnel cloud is considered a mature tornado when it touches the ground, but it doesn't have a very long life. A study of 20,000 twisters showed an average life span of just 15 minutes. For 7 to 10 minutes, the tornado is usually straight up-and-down. Then it begins to tilt and twist like a rope. Sometimes a tornado ends by flipping up and reattaching itself to the cloud. When it disappears, the tremendous shower of dust and debris it has been carrying falls to the ground.

EXPERIMENT

STORMY WEATHER ON THE STOVETOP!

Clashes of cold and warm air can churn out winds that make up Earth's deadliest storms. This activity shows how different temperatures make liquids and gases in the air move. **You will need an adult to help you.**

What You Need:
- A flameproof glass cake or bread pan

- Food coloring

What to Do:
1. Ask an adult to help you at the stove.
2. Fill the pan with water and place only one end of it over a small burner.
3. Turn the burner on to the lowest setting.
4. Add two drops of food coloring to the cool end of the pan.
5. Watch the pan from the side.

What Happens and Why:
The colored water moves down and toward the warm end, then rises upward and back toward the cool end. This movement, which occurs in the air during stormy weather, is called a **convection current**. Convection is motion between liquids or gases of different temperatures. This motion can become fast and furious in the sky, resulting in thunderstorms, damaging winds, and tornadoes.

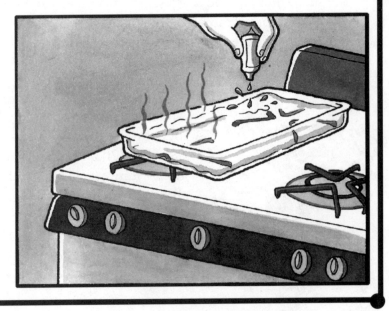

Tornado Myths

Tornadoes have blown around a lot of folklore that just isn't true. Let's sort out the fact from the fiction:

Myth: Areas near rivers, lakes, and mountains are safe from tornadoes.

Fact: No place is safe from tornadoes! In the late 1980s, a tornado tore a path of destruction up and down a 10,000-foot mountain in Yellowstone National Park.

Myth: The pressure within a tornado causes buildings to explode.

Fact: Most damage is caused by violent winds and debris slamming into buildings.

Myth: Windows should be opened to equalize pressure in the house during a tornado.

Fact: Opening windows only lets damaging winds enter the building. Leave the windows alone; instead, get to a safe spot inside the house immediately.

Tornado Warning, Tornado Watch

With all its high-tech equipment, the National Weather Service is very good at tracking and warning us about storms that can produce tornadoes. When conditions in a certain area are right for the formation of tornadoes, they issue a **tornado watch**. However, it's impossible to know if tornadoes actually will form until one is spotted. Then the National Weather Service issues a **tornado warning**.

If you hear a tornado watch, keep the radio or television on for further information. If a tornado warning has been issued for your area, take shelter immediately! The safest shelters are basements or interior rooms without any windows. In any case, you are always safer inside than outside, where the wind and the objects carried by it are very dangerous.

The World's Worst Tornado

On March 18, 1925, the deadliest single tornado in U.S. history ripped a 219-mile (352-km) path from Ellington, Missouri, to Petersburg, Indiana. Along the way it killed 689 people, gave 2,000 people serious injuries, and left 8,000 people homeless.

Policeman Joe Boston of Murphysboro, Illinois, experienced one of the more bizarre tricks of the killer tornado. Before the twister hit, he had an important document, a bond for a deed, locked inside a safe in his home. When the tornado passed over, it sucked the paper out of the safe (the door never opened) and transported it 125 miles (200 km) to the town of Lawrenceville, where a good citizen found it and mailed it back to Mr. Boston!

6

Frozen Stuff
WHEN WEATHER GETS FLAKY

Where I grew up near Richmond, Virginia, the average snowfall is only 14.6 inches (37 centimeters) per year. So a big snowstorm was a rare and much-welcomed event. We'd get a day off from school and have a big outdoor party of sledding and snowman making and **snowball fights** that I wished would never end.

Now, after twenty-five years as a weather reporter, I know that snow can also cause serious hardships for a lot of people. In the brutal, record-setting winter of 1995–1996, the snowstorms that hit the northern United States kept coming and coming, and I came under attack from practically everybody after each one of them! Fortunately, I still find something beautiful and wonderful about snow. Let's explore the natural processes that produce frozen precipitation.

What Is Snow?

When a cloud becomes cold enough (less than 32° Fahrenheit or 0° Celsius—the freezing point of water), it creates snowflakes instead of rain. Snowflakes are made of crystals.

Like raindrops, the snow crystals begin with a tiny water droplet that condenses on a speck of dust or other airborne matter. The water droplet then freezes, becoming a tiny piece of ice that acts as a seed to which more droplets can cling. If the cloud these droplets are in is less than 32° Fahrenheit, the droplets freeze to form snow crystals. Because of the way water molecules fit together, most snowflakes are 𝕤𝕚𝕩-𝕤𝕚𝕕𝕖𝕕, or hexagonal. When they get heavy enough, the snowflakes fall to Earth, sometimes in clusters of hundreds of flakes—and we have snow.

The Man Who Loved Snowflakes

The first person to get really serious about sketching and photographing snowflakes was a young American scientist from Vermont named Wilson A. Bentley. In 1880, he purchased a microscope and used it to examine a snowflake. He expected to see a tiny chunk of ice. Instead, what he saw through the eyepiece was an incredibly delicate, beautiful, six-sided sculpture formed from ice crystals. The sight was so breathtaking that Bentley rigged up a camera to take a picture through the microscope so he could have a permanent record of it.

O ver the next forty years, "Snowflake" Bentley, as he came to be called, took more than 5,000 pictures of snowflakes, which he organized into more than eighty different types. In addition to variations of the flat, lacy, six-sided snowflakes that we always see in pictures, his lens also captured flakes shaped like needles, hollow columns, and capped columns.

Scientists later created a system for classifying the different types of snowflakes, and discovered that different conditions in the clouds are responsible for these different shapes. The following chart shows the seven main types of snowflakes. Some of them may look more familiar to you than others. If you catch any snowflake in your hand or on the tip of your finger, take a very quick look because the warmth of your skin will melt the flake in a flash! The very smallest, really tiny flakes are known as **diamond dust**.

The shape of a snowflake is determined by where it forms in the cloud. In the highest clouds, where the temperature is coldest, snowflakes take the shape of six-sided columns, sometimes with caps on the ends that make them look like little spools. Slightly warmer temperatures in middle cloud layers give snowflakes both a column form and a flat, six-sided shape called a hexagonal plate. The lowest clouds, where the temperature is warmer, breed snowflakes in many shapes: hexagonal plates, short columns, long thin needles, and stars.

Is It True That No Two Snowflakes Are Alike?

There's no scientific reason why two snowflakes can't be identical. But because the average snowflake is made up of 180 billion molecules of water, with billions of possible ways of connecting to each other, the odds of two snowflakes being identical twins are very, very low. In all of his years of study, Mr. Bentley never found two snowflakes that looked alike.

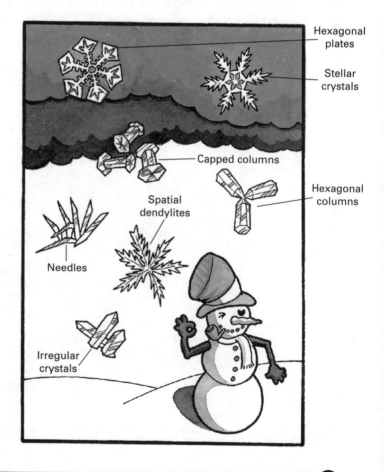

Hexagonal plates

Stellar crystals

Capped columns

Hexagonal columns

Spatial dendylites

Needles

Irregular crystals

EXPERIMENT

BE A SNOWFLAKE GAZER

The next time it snows in your town, or when you take a trip to the mountains, here's a simple way to catch snowflakes and get a close-up look at their delicate structure and variety of design.

What You Need:
• A piece of black felt or cardboard, about 4" square

• A magnifying glass

What to Do:
1. Put your black square in the refrigerator for a few minutes before you go outside so that the snowflakes won't melt on it.
2. Once outside, hold out the square until a few flakes fall on it. Use your magnifying glass to observe the details of a snowflake's shape. Refer to the snowflake name chart on page 73. How many different types of snowflakes can you find?

Snow Q & A: Answers to Some Sticky Questions

How big do snowflakes get?

Although the average snowflake measures less than a half-inch (1.3 centimeters) in diameter, observers have captured giant snowflakes ranging from 3 to 4 inches (8 to 10 centimeters)—longer than your finger!

Why is snow white when an ice cube is clear?

Snowflakes are made up of many ice crystals, each of which has many different surfaces that act like tiny mirrors. Light doesn't pass straight through, but bounces off all the surfaces to make the snowflake appear white.

How do we measure snow?

You might imagine that scientists have come up with some complicated instrument for measuring snow. Actually, you just stick a yardstick or ruler into snow in an area not affected by blowing or drifting.

Why does snow melt when it first hits the ground, then start sticking?

When the weather turns colder, the air loses heat faster than the ground does. If the ground temperature remains slightly above freezing, the first snowflakes will melt. However, this melting of falling snow quickly cools the ground, and when the temperature drops below freezing, the snow starts to stick.

Why does salt melt snow and ice?

The chemical name for salt is sodium chloride, and when it comes in contact with water, it breaks up into sodium and chloride molecules. These molecules act like magnets for water molecules, which are more attracted to the sodium and chloride than they are to each other. This "fatal attraction" means that water molecules won't join together to form ice crystals. However, salt doesn't break down into sodium and chloride when the temperatures are too cold, which is why it won't melt the ice on your sidewalk when the thermometer plunges towards zero.

How much water is in snow?

Scientists determine how much water snow holds by measuring the depth of snow in a container, then melting it to measure the amount of water. On the average, 10 inches of snow is equivalent to 1 inch of rain. However, that inch of water might come from 6 inches of very wet snow or 12 inches of very light, puffy snow.

Can it ever be too cold to snow?

Where do you think it snows the most—at the North Pole or in Buffalo, New York? The answer may surprise you. The colder the air, the less water vapor it can hold, and as we just learned, it's the water vapor in clouds that forms snow crystals. For this reason, Buffalo gets much more snow than either the North or South Pole, where the ultracold temperatures prevent snow from forming. In North America, the snowiest areas are throughout most of Canada and the top third of the United States.

The Windchill Factor

In the winter, cold temperatures can feel even colder in a strong wind. When the wind hits your body, you lose heat more quickly than you would if the air was calm. Your body must work harder to keep warm because the wind brings more cold air to your skin before it has a chance to warm up. The windchill is the colder temperature you feel. For example, if you're outside on a day when the temperature of the air is 25° Fahrenheit (-4° Celsius) and the wind is blowing at 20 miles (32 km) per hour, the air feels like it's -3° Fahrenheit (-20° Celsius).

Blizzards and Nor'easters

A storm that results when a low-pressure system moves along the east coast is called a **nor'easter**, because the winds come from the northeast. The air in low-pressure systems spins counterclockwise, and pulls in tremendous amounts of moisture from the Atlantic Ocean into the air above land. Nor'easters bring by far the heaviest snows to New England and the Middle Atlantic states along with near hurricane force winds.

When all the ingredients are just right, nature can produce a severe winter storm that can stop a city in its tracks. A **blizzard** is defined as a storm system with the three following aspects:

- Gale-force winds of 35 miles per hour (56 km/hour) or more
- Temperatures below 20° Fahrenheit (-7° Celsius)
- Blowing snow

Does it seem that something is missing from the list? What about a high rate of snowfall? The power and danger of a blizzard comes from snow being driven by great winds, and this can happen with snow that is already on the ground, not just with new snow. In the Antarctic, where it's common for winds to reach speeds of 90 miles per hour (145 km/hour), ice particles from the hard-packed surface are swept up into the air to produce the most dangerous blizzards on Earth.

Other Kinds of Frozen Precipitation

In addition to snow, we're also sometimes subjected to sleet, freezing rain, and hail. Sleet and freezing rain occur when temperatures are hovering around the freezing mark. Hail, on the other hand, falls only from giant thunderclouds that form during the warmer months of the year.

Sleet, or Rain That Hurts

Sleet is made of tiny balls of ice that form when raindrops freeze as they fall into a band of below-freezing air near the ground. The easiest way to tell sleet from snow is that sleet bounces when it hits the ground. If it's windy and sleeting, the icy little particles can sting when they hit your face. In very unstable air, it is possible for rain, sleet, and snow to fall at the same time.

Reading the Rings

Every time a hailstone is tossed back up into a stormcloud, it gathers another layer of ice. This makes a hailstone look a lot like an onion, and if you cut a big one in half you can clearly see its rings. By counting them, you can discover how many trips the hailstone made up into the cloud.

Freezing Rain

Freezing rain occurs when the air temperature is above freezing but the ground temperature is below freezing. In these conditions, raindrops hit the ground and instantly freeze, forming a layer of ice on roads, trees, and power lines. Fortunately, these conditions usually don't last very long before the precipitation turns to all rain or all snow. The relatively rare ice storms that result when freezing rain falls for hours are the most dangerous of all winter precipitation. Roads turn to ice and the clear, heavy glaze that covers the trees and power lines can bring them crashing to the ground.

Hail, or Rain That *Really* Hurts

Hail is the only frozen precipitation that forms in warm weather. It is produced by the powerful thunderstorms that result when a cold front clashes with a warm front. The precipitation in thunderclouds, as we've learned, starts as ice crystals formed high in the clouds. These crystals attract water droplets to form raindrops and melt as they fall towards Earth. However, in certain thunderstorms, the upward air currents are so strong that ice crystals that are starting to melt are blown back up several thousand feet into the colder air, where another layer of ice forms around them. The crystals bounce up and down, as if they're on a trampoline of air, growing bigger and bigger. When the crystals finally become so heavy that gravity is stronger than the upward currents, they fall to the ground as pellets of ice we call hail. Wind patterns usually form hailstones into balls, but they can also appear in the shape of cones, discs, stars, pyramids, or simply weird, pointy blobs.

Hail That Made History

The largest hailstone ever officially measured weighed 1.67 pounds (.75 kilograms) and measured 17.5 inches (44.5 centimeters) around. About the size of a grapefruit, it was found in Coffeyville, Kansas, in 1970.

Hundreds of English solders were killed near Paris in 1360 when hailstones the size of goose eggs fell from the sky.

Hundreds of cattle, sheep, and goats and 246 people died in a storm that sent down hailstones the size of "cricket balls" near New Delhi, India, in 1888.

On June 19, 1932, in Honan Province, China, a hailstorm passed over 400 villages, destroying houses and crops and killing 200 people.

A hailstorm in a northern region of South Africa in 1936 left the ground covered with jagged lumps of ice 3 feet deep.

The more violent the thunderstorm, the stronger the updrafts and the larger the hail. Although most hailstones measure less than an inch in diameter, **golfball-size** hail is not unusual in "Hail Alley," the area made up of northern Colorado, southeastern Wyoming, and western Nebraska that gets hail nine or ten times every year. This area, as well as the Eastern Rocky Mountains and the Great Plains, experiences the most destructive hail in the nation. Hail falls in many countries, including Greece, France, and the Commonwealth of Independent States. But the world's worst hail zone is in the Kericho and Nandi hills of Kenya, Africa, where it hails about 132 days per year. Hail *doesn't* fall in the tropics, where thunderstorm clouds are too warm to create the ice balls.

Weather at Its Weirdest: The Case of the Human Hailstone!

A bizarre event that occurred in Germany in 1930 gives us a terrifying look at the enormous forces at work in a storm system. As sixteen glider pilots flew in a contest to see who could reach the highest altitude, strong winds carried them into storm clouds that were forming over the mountains. Sensing the danger of the powerful updraft, fourteen of the pilots quickly steered their planes out of the current and out of trouble. But two pilots were pulled into the system and trapped in currents of swirling air that lifted them up 40,000 feet (12,192 meters). Their gliders were blasted apart by the winds, and both pilots tried to parachute down to safety. One made it. The other was carried up into a cloud, where layers of ice froze on him. He then fell 7 miles to his death—a human hailstone!

The path in which hail falls is known as a **hailstreak,** and it usually covers an area from 100 yards to 2 miles (91 meters to 3.2 kilometers) wide, and about 5 miles (8 kilometers) long. However, giant storms have left hailstreaks 50 miles wide and 200 miles long (80 by 322 kilometers).

People who live in hail country don't need a weather forecaster like me to tell them there's a chance of hail. They know exactly what to look for in the sky. Thunderclouds that cast a dark blue-green color, much like the clouds that spawn tornadoes, are a sure sign of hail.

Glaciers: Nature's Biggest Ice

A glacier is a large mass of ice that forms in an area where less snow melts in the summer than falls in the winter. Over hundreds and thousands of years, the weight of the snow on top presses down on the snow below and compacts it into ice.

The two largest glaciers are the polar ice caps that cover 5 million square miles (13 million square kilometers—95 percent of the land surface) of Antarctica and 1.8 million square miles (5 million square kilometers) of Greenland. These gigantic masses of ice are more than 9,000 feet (2,743 meters) thick.

Glaciers are found in the mountainous regions of every continent except Australia.

How Do Glaciers Move?

Try rubbing one hand back and forth rapidly on your arm. The friction produces heat. When the height of a glacier gets to 100 feet or more, the weight of the ice creates friction with the ground, causing heat that melts a layer of ice close to the ground. The pressure of additional falling snow causes the glacier to slide along on the layer of melted water beneath it. Although the average speed of a glacier is 3 feet per day, speeds of up to 100 feet per day have been recorded.

Without an increase in snowfall, however, a glacier shrinks.

Icebergs: Floating Mountains

Most **icebergs** are giant chunks that break off from the glaciers covering Greenland or Antarctica and float off into the ocean. About 90 percent of the mass of an iceberg is below the surface of the water, so an iceberg is a floating ice mountain 300 to 500 feet (91 to 152 meters) high that extends 2,700 to 4,500 feet (823 to 1,372 meters) into the ocean depths. The largest iceberg ever spotted was as large as the state of Rhode Island. Icebergs can float 2,000 miles (3,220 kilometers) or more before melting. Because they consist of fresh (not salt) water, some people have proposed towing icebergs to serve as water sources for such dry areas as Southern California.

7

Songbirds and Satellites

HOW ANIMALS AND INSTRUMENTS HELP US FORECAST THE WEATHER

If you have watched a weather broadcast recently (I hope it was on **Good Morning America!**), you've probably noticed that a lot of high technology is available to people who forecast the weather. This technology includes satellite photography (regular and infrared), normal radar, Doppler radar, and weather balloons.

Every day, thousands of weather observation stations scattered across the United States send hourly reports to the National Weather Service in Washingon, D.C. About a hundred of these stations get their information

from **radiosondes**, packages of weather instruments that are lifted many miles into the air by weather balloons. This constant, enormous stream of information is fed into the National Weather Service computer system, where it is analyzed to prepare short- and long-range forecasts for every part of the country.

Now, let's go back in time about 50,000 years, long before any civilizations developed, when a lot of our ancestors were living in caves. These early humans were just as concerned about the weather as we are today—it affected their daily plans for hunting, gathering food, and other outdoor activities. Long before the invention of weather instruments, people spent a great deal of time observing nature. Gradually, people learned to link the direction of the wind, the type and movement of clouds, the behavior of animals, and the position of the stars to certain types of weather.

The scientific study of weather began in the 1600's, when weather instruments were invented. In this chapter, we're going to explore the subject of weather instruments, both natural and manufactured. We'll show you how you can use simple instruments and simple observations to produce your own forecasts.

Measuring Temperature

One of the most useful things to know about the weather is how hot or cold it is outside. If you're deciding whether to wear shorts or a sweater to school, you're likely to glance at a **thermometer**, the most common of all weather instruments.

VERY HOT

BODY TEMPERATURE

+122 / +50

+104 / +40
+98.6 / +37

+86 / +30

ROOM TEMPERATURE

+68 / +20

+50 / +10

+32 / 0 — FREEZING POINT

+14 / -10

BITTER COLD -4 / -20

EXTREME COLD -22 / -30

°F / °C
Fahrenheit / Celsius

Who Invented the Thermometer?

The first thermometer was invented by the great Italian scientist Galileo (1564–1642). Galileo was interested in physics, and he discovered that liquids expanded when they were warmed. In 1612, he sealed some colored alcohol in a glass tube with a round ball at the bottom. As the temperature rose, the alcohol expanded to move up the tube. The level of the alcohol rose and fell with the temperature, making it the very first thermometer. For the next two hundred years, scientists throughout Europe experimented with different liquids in the thermometer. For a long time, the most popular type of liquid was **wine**. But experiments using mercury showed better results, because mercury remained liquid at temperatures that would freeze wine, and it did not evaporate at high temperatures. Gradually, mercury won out over every other type of thermometer.

As great an invention as the thermometer was, there was a still a major problem: How do you develop a consistent scale of measurement so that the temperatures in two places could be compared accurately? Think of trying to measure the length of a room without a yardstick or tape measure. You could use the length of your foot, the length of your stride, or the length of your **cat's tail**. But whatever measurement you came up with wouldn't mean a thing to someone with a different-size foot, a different-size stride, or a different-size cat.

For a hundred years, scientists experimented with scales based on everything from the temperature of melting butter to the temperature of the blood of various animals. Finally, in 1714, a German scientist came up with the first scale that was widely used. His name was Gabriel Daniel Fahrenheit.

What Is the Fahrenheit Scale?

To create his temperature scale, Fahrenheit used the coldest substance he could find, a water-ice-salt mixture, for the fixed point of 0°. As his second fixed point, he used the temperature of human blood. He divided the interval between these two points into 96 equal parts, or degrees. Using this scale, the temperature of the freezing point of water became 32° and the temperature at which water boiled was 212°.

Centigrade and Kelvin Temperature Scales

To improve on Fahrenheit's rather unscientific temperature scale, a Swedish astronomer named Anders Celsius came up with a more rational scale in 1742. He made 0° the freezing point of water and 100° the boiling point of water. This scale, called the Centigrade or **Celsius scale**, is used by many scientists and most countries in the world.

Lord Kelvin, a British scientist, came up with the most detailed of all scales in 1850. He assigned 0° to the point where it is so cold that all molecular action stops. This "absolute zero" is −459.2° Fahrenheit and −273.18° Celsius. Water freezes at 273° Kelvin and boils at 373° Kelvin. The **Kelvin scale** is used exclusively by scientists.

How Do Temperature Changes Predict the Weather?

Temperatures are normally at their lowest just before dawn. They rise after sunrise, peak in mid-afternoon, then gradually descend again as darkness falls. Any interruptions in this pattern means that the weather is about to change. For example, a sharp drop in temperature in the morning can signal the arrival of a cold front, which could produce precipitation shortly. On the other hand, as Native American tribes discovered, a rise in temperature between 9 P.M. and midnight signals the more gradual arrival of a warm front, which will probably produce rain by the next morning.

Natural Thermometers

By far the most accurate natural thermometer is the cricket. To find out what the temperature is, count the number of chirps a cricket produces in exactly 30 seconds, then add 37. For example, if a cricket chirps 40 times, add 37, and you arrive at a temperature of 77° Fahrenheit. I know it sounds strange, but try it—you'll be surprised!

Measuring Air Pressure

Galileo was the first scientist to discover that air has weight, but it was an assistant of his named Evangelista Torricelli who came up with a way to measure that weight. Torricelli was fascinated by a mystery: No matter how much suction was used, water from a well couldn't be raised more than 34 feet. He finally decided that the reason was the air pressure, which meant that the level of water in a pipe would rise and fall as the air pressure rose and fell.

Because working with a 34-foot-tall pipe was impossible, Torricelli decided to use **mercury**, which is fourteen times denser than water. (A given volume of mercury is fourteen times heavier than the same volume of water.) He filled a glass bowl with mercury, into which he inserted a glass tube sealed at the top. Air pressure on the surface of the mercury outside the glass forced mercury up the glass tube about 30 inches. Over time, the height of the mercury rose and fell with the air pressure.

This instrument for measuring air pressure, as we learned in chapter 1, is called a **barometer**. To this day we still use inches of mercury as our scale.

How Do Changes in Air Pressure Help Us Forecast the Weather?

As a budding weather expert, you've learned that low-pressure systems bring storms and high-pressure systems bring fair weather. Air pressure changes are the most reliable indicators of what changes are likely to take place in the weather over the short term. Rising air pressure means better weather. A falling barometer reading, on the other hand, means a storm is coming. The lower the air pressure, the more severe the storm—hurricanes have the lowest pressure of any type of system.

Natural Barometers

Because they are very sensitive to changes in air pressure, animals react to low pressure, becoming living, breathing barometers!

For countless centuries, hunters, herdsmen, farmers, and fishermen have been able to detect changes in animal behavior when the air pressure lowers, and read them as signs that a storm is on the way. In colonial times, cats were considered important four-footed weather forecasters, and were respected by everyone from housewives to Benjamin Franklin. If a cat left its perch on the windowsill or other favorite spot and curled up in a more protected spot in the house, its owners expected that foul weather would soon follow.

When I was a kid, the cats in our neighborhood would act very strangely before a big storm, running around in circles and making weird screaming sounds. My mother used them as barometers of how severe a storm would be—the stranger they

acted, the worse the storm would be. Sometimes, as a thunderstorm moved closer and closer, the electrical charge in the air would make the cats' fur stand straight on end!

Here are more examples of how animals behave when the air pressure suddenly drops:

- Birds fly low, for two reasons: the lower air pressure in the upper air hurts their ears, and it also keeps the insects they hunt closer to the ground.
- Horses, cows, and sheep become restless and herd closer together.
- Ducks, geese, and sea birds stay on the ground because the lower air pressure makes it more difficult to glide on air currents.
- Frogs croak loudly and don't leave the water.

- Fish, dolphins, and whales swim closer to the surface.
- Ants build and reinforce their nests, so fresh dirt on an anthill is a sign that a storm is coming.
  - All insects become more active.

The Famous Weather-Forecasting Goats of Mt. Nebo

From about 1965 to 1979 a herd of goats grazed on Mt. Nebo near Roseburg, Oregon. Local people who watched the mountainside every day noticed that the weather was fair and dry when the goats were on the higher part of the mountain, and overcast or rainy when the goats were grazing on the lower slopes. When the local radio station began giving the daily Goat Weather Forecast, news spread about the clever herd. The radio station made a comparison of the goats' behavior and the Weather Bureau forecasts, and discovered that the goats, who were right 90 percent of the time, beat out the pros, who were only 65 percent

accurate! At the height of their fame, the goats were featured on national television and in magazines and newspapers around the world.

WEATHER REPORT

50   25   30

75   60   80

EXPERIMENT

HAIR HYGROMETER

In case you miss the weather report, you can get a simple reading of the relative humidity yourself with a hygrometer that uses a strand of your own hair.

What You Need:
- Pencil

- 2 index cards

- Paper hole-punch

- Scissors

- Paper fastener

- 1 strand of your hair

- Ruler

- Masking tape

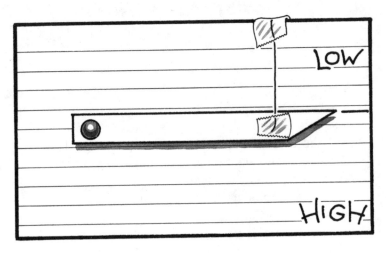

What to Do:
1. With the pencil, mark a spot on one of the index cards halfway down the short side of the card and about 1 inch (2.5 cm) in from the edge.
2. Punch a hole in the card where you marked the spot.
3. From the second card, cut a thin strip from the long side that is a bit wider than the hole in the first card.
4. Cut one end of the strip at an angle to make a point.
5. At the other end of the strip, punch a hole
6. Attach the strip to the first card with the paper fastener through the holes.
7. Take a 4-inch-long (10 cm) strand of hair from your head, or, if your hair is too short, from a friend with longer hair. Attach one end of the hair to the pointed end of the strip with tape.
8. Tape the other end of the hair to the top of the card, or if it's longer, to the back, so that the strip is suspended and points to the middle of the card.
9. Mark the spot at the edge of the card that the strip is pointing to.
10. Above this mark, write the word "Low," and below the mark write "High."

continued

EXPERIMENT

continued

11. Place your hygrometer outside.
12. Check the hygrometer every day and mark where the arrow points.

What Happens and Why:
The more water vapor in the air, the more your hair will soak up. As it does, it lengthens and the arrow falls toward the "High" area. This shows the air has become more humid. When there is less water vapor in the air, the strand of hair will dry and shrink, moving the pointer to the "Low" area. You'll find that the greater the relative humidity, the longer your hair; the lower the relative humidity, the shorter your hair becomes.

Measuring Humidity

Have you ever tied your **shoelaces** when they were wet, then tried to untie them when they were dry? I'll bet that they were very difficult to untie, because they tightened as they dried. Almost everything that absorbs water expands when it is wet and shrinks when it dries.

Hundreds of years ago, scientists used this fact to measure **humidity,** the amount of water vapor in the air. Scientists observed that when the humidity was high, human hair, horse hair, and thread absorbed moisture and got longer. When the air dried, the hair or thread got shorter. In 1743, some Italian scientists invented an instrument, called a hair **hygrometer,** that gave a rough indication of humidity by measuring how much a single human hair expanded or shrunk. Today, you can still buy (or make) hygrometers that use hair or paper to measure **relative humidity,** the amount of water vapor in the air compared to maximum amount of water vapor that air can possibly hold. If the relative humidity is 100 percent, the air contains all the water vapor that it can hold.

Humidity is an important part of weather forecasting. In order for rain or other precipitation to fall, the humidity has to be high. If the air is dry, any precipitation will evaporate before it reaches the ground. If the relative humidity is below 50 percent, you can put away the umbrellas and snow shovels. If the relative humidity climbs above 75 or 80 percent, expect precipitation soon.

Nature's Humidity Indicators

Many plants are sensitive to the amount of moisture in the air. When the humidity is high, the flowers of many plants close up to protect their pollen from being washed away. The leaves of many different kinds of trees curl up and expose their undersides when damp air arrives. On the other hand, the pitcher plant opens its mouth wide when the humidity is high, and toadstools and mushrooms start to release their spores.

Stones, brick, and metal objects seem to sweat in high humidity. Wood beams and furniture swell when the air is moist, causing floors and chairs to creak. Also, smoke from a fire or chimney rises straight upward in dry air, but picks up moisture and drifts toward the ground on damp days.

Measuring Wind Direction and Speed

Wind direction must have been one of the first weather observations made by early humans. They would have wanted to know, for example, that they were downwind from an animal they were hunting so that it couldn't smell them coming. By throwing a handful of dust or leaves into the air, these early meteorologists could figure out from which direction the wind was blowing. The ancient Greeks and Romans used weather vanes, pointers that would swivel as wind direction changed, to find the direction of the wind. Today, we still use weather vanes or wind socks.

It wasn't until 1667 that scientists developed the first **anemometer,** a device that measures the speed of the wind. The most common type of anemometer used today is sort of like a pinwheel, with rotating cups that catch the wind. The rate of spinning indicates the wind speed.

Why Are Roosters Portrayed on So Many Weather Vanes?

The custom of designing weather vanes shaped like roosters dates back to an order issued by a pope in the ninth century. Because St. Peter denied that he knew Jesus Christ three times before the rooster crowed, the pope ordered that the image of a rooster be placed on weather vanes to remind people about temptation. Even though the religious purpose was forgotten long ago, the custom of putting a rooster on a weather vane is still popular today.

How Wind Aids Weather Forecasting

Remember the eight-sided Tower of the Winds built in Athens that was described in chapter 1? In addition to naming the eight wind directions, the Greeks and Romans also linked certain types of weather with wind direction, something we continue to do today. For example, in the northeastern United States, northwest winds bring bitterly cold arctic weather, while southwestern winds bring warm, moist air.

In each area of the United States, meteorologists use wind direction to make forecasts. In one Connecticut city, for example, local meteorologists have developed this formula: a northeast wind means a 76-percent chance of precipitation in the next 24 hours, while a northwest wind brings only a 34-percent chance of

The anemometer measures the speed of the wind.

in the next 24 hours, while a northwest wind brings only a 34-percent chance of precipitation in winter and a 16-percent chance in summer.

What does wind speed tell us about the weather? We know that the greater the differences in air pressure between two air masses, the greater the wind speed. Therefore, higher wind speeds indicate rapid and dramatic changes in weather patterns.

The Beaufort Scale

You don't need an anemometer to estimate wind speed. Instead, you can use a system developed by British Admiral Francis Beaufort in 1805. This system, called the Beaufort Scale, uses your powers of observation to determine the speed of the wind. Here is a simplified version of his scale:

The Beaufort Wind Scale

Less than 1 mph
Smoke rises

1–3 mph
Smoke drifts

4–7 mph
Leaves rustle slightly and flags stir

8–12 mph
Leaves and twigs move

13–18 mph
Small branches move and flags flap

19–24 mph
Small trees sway and flags ripple

25–31 mph
Large branches move and flags beat

32–38 mph
Whole trees move and flags extend

39–46 mph
Twigs break and walking is difficult

47–54 mph
Signs and antennas blow down

55–73 mph
Trees uprooted; damage to buildings

74+ mph
Devastation to countryside (hurricane)

Basic Weather Forecasting

To make a complete forecast, you need to get information about six aspects of the weather: sky conditions, cloud cover, temperature, humidity, air pressure, and wind direction. With just a few simple gadgets, anyone can become an amateur weather forecaster.

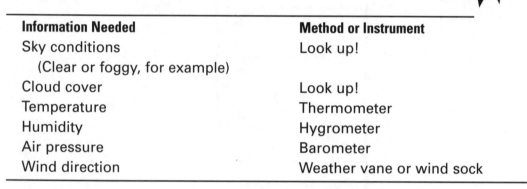

Information Needed	Method or Instrument
Sky conditions (Clear or foggy, for example)	Look up!
Cloud cover	Look up!
Temperature	Thermometer
Humidity	Hygrometer
Air pressure	Barometer
Wind direction	Weather vane or wind sock

You can learn to forecast short-term changes in the weather accurately by making these simple observations. You've already learned what kind of weather comes with different types of clouds (in chapter 2). Add to this the measurements from the instruments in the above chart, and follow these general weather guidelines to make your forecast:

What You Observe	What It Means
Rising air pressure	Fair weather
Less humidity	Fair weather
Signs of lower air pressure	Precipitation (rain, snow)
Higher humidity	Precipitation (rain, snow)

Create your own weather journal, writing down weather conditions and the weather that shortly follows, and you'll soon be able to gain confidence in your new skill by comparing your results with the local TV or radio weather forecasts.

Weather Symbols

The weather maps used on television and published in newspapers all over the world, contain standard weather symbols. These symbols make it easy to aborb a lot of information at a glance.

Knowing what the weather is going to be like makes life easier for all of us. Accurate weather reports are serious business to those whose work depends on them, like pilots, sailors, and farmers. And by applying the latest technology to modern weather forecasting, meteorologists are able to track severe storms and hurricanes and give people time to prepare for them—an important advancement in science that has saved many lives.

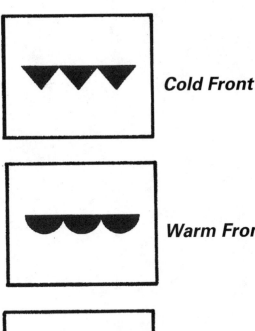

Cold Front

Warm Front

Stationary Front

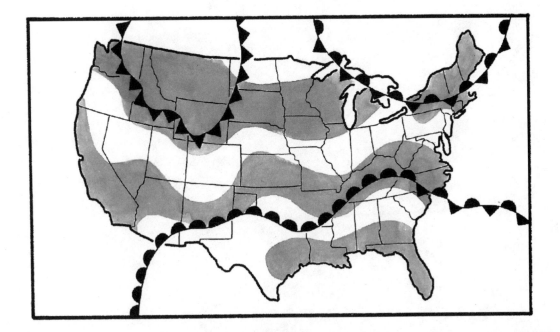

8

Groundhogs, Shadows, and Silly Sayings

THE TRUTH ABOUT WEATHER LORE

I have a very positive attitude toward life, but there is one day each year on which it's a little harder to get out of bed in the morning—February 2. The reason: it's **Groundhog Day**, and I know that *Good Morning America* and nearly every other national and local news program will have cameras waiting to record whether or not a groundhog sees its shadow. Inevitably, dozens of people will ask me, "Spencer, how come a groundhog knows how long winter will last and you don't?" What they're really saying is, "Spencer, how come you're dumber than a groundhog?" I'm tempted to reply, "If you think groundhogs are so smart, why don't you let one take your next math test?"

The truth is, ground-hogs aren't smarter than meteorologists (though they may be cuter). Scientific studies have shown absolutely no correlation between a groundhog seeing its shadow and the length of a winter. But just because groundhog forecasting is a **myth**, it doesn't mean that all weather sayings aren't true. Many observations of nature do provide information about weather events. However, along with the wisdom is a lot of superstition. I think you'll enjoy discovering which weather sayings have some basis in truth and which are fiction.

If It Happened Once, It Will Happen Again

For many centuries, English farmers believed that the weather in the month of February somehow sets the pattern for the weather for the rest of the year. For some reason, they settled on February 2, which they called Candlemas Day, as the most significant day in determining how long winter would last. Our Groundhog Day myth comes from this colorful but meaningless English tradition. Here are some sayings based on patterns:

The first frost in autumn will be exactly six months after the first thunderstorm of the spring.

As many days old as is the moon on the day of the first snow, there will be that many snowfalls by crop planting time.

My job as a weather forecaster would be very easy if these sayings were true: six months after the first autumn frost, I'd know there would be a thunderstorm. Unfortunately, sayings based on continuation of patterns have no basis in fact.

For Every Wrong, There's a Right

From ancient times to the modern day, many people have wanted to believe that there was some sort of force, natural or supernatural, that balanced good weather and bad weather. For example, a hard winter should be followed by a warm, sunny spring, and if it rained on your birthday last year, it should be dry and pleasant this year. Many weather sayings have been built on this belief, such as:

If March comes in like a lamb, it will go out like a lion.

A warm Christmas, a cold Easter.

Nice as this idea is, no one seems to have convinced Mother Nature. Weather history is filled with long droughts, extended series of wet summers, and even ice ages that lasted tens of thousands of years. That's why long-range weather forecasting is such a challenge.

Watching the Sky and the Clouds

Red sky at night, sailors' delight;
Red sky in morning, sailors take warning.

Of all weather sayings, the oldest and most reliable are those such as this one that involve observations of the sky and clouds. In this case, the old folklore is based on a solid fact: weather basically moves from west to east. In order for the sun to reflect from clouds, the western horizon must be clear, which means fair skies will probably move in. On the other hand, a red sunrise means that sunlight is reflecting from high clouds moving in from the west, clouds that are often forerunners of storm systems.

Sharks as Weather Forecasters?

Sharks have been used to predict the weather. In Bermuda, some fishermen still use a 300-year-old method of weather forecasting based on shark oil. Tradition calls for oil from a shark that is captured during either the first quarter of the moon or the full moon, between the months of June and September. This is the time when the shark's liver contains the most fat. The fat is heated and strained to get the oil. Those who read the shark oil to predict the weather claim that when the oil is perfectly clear, the weather will be fair. When the oil gets cloudy or solid particles form in it, the shark oil reader studies the changes in the oil to predict wind, rain, or storms.

Could a Caterpillar Steal My Job?

We learned in chapter 7 that many animals are sensitive to changes in air pressure, and that their behavior can help predict if a storm is near. For this reason, many people believe that animals can be long-range weather forecasters, too. For example, many people believe that the winter will be cold and snowy if:

• Squirrels accumulate huge stores of nuts

- The brown stripes on the backs of woolly bear caterpillars are broader than the black stripes
- Beavers build heavier lodges than usual
- Hair on bears and horses is thick early in the autumn
- The breastbone of a fresh-cooked turkey is dark purple

Unfortunately, none of these predicters are true. For example, the pattern of stripes on woolly bears is determined by genetics and the environmental conditions in which the insect grows, not on what's coming up in the future. Similarly, horses and bears may grow thicker hair if October and November are cold, but that doesn't necessarily mean that the rest of the winter will be cold.

Come to Your Senses!

Today, we use computers to generate the information on which we base our weather forecasts, but long ago, people relied a lot more on their five senses. Here are some sayings based on our senses:

The squeak of the snow will the temperature show.

Ditches and manure piles smell stronger just before it rains.

Sound travels far and wide, a stormy day will betide.

The farther the sight, the nearer the rain.

Why are these sayings true? Let's take sound first. Generally, the higher the humidity, the better sound travels. In some English cities, people judged the chances of rain by how clearly they could hear the church bells ring. The sound of our footsteps on snow also helps us guess the temperature—the louder the squeak, the colder the air.

Another common saying is true—we can "smell" rain, even though water vapor has no odor. How? Well, plants exude oils that are absorbed by the soil. When the air pressure drops, the soil releases some of these oils, producing a smell we've learned to interpret as the "smell of rain." Dropping air pressure also brings out the odors of flowers and manure more strongly.

Since the beginning of recorded history, people have noted that faraway objects appear closer before a storm. The reason is a difference in the temperatures between levels of air as a storm approaches. These temperatures cause light to be refracted in a way that makes faraway objects appear closer.

Finally, weather also seems to affect our moods. A combination of low air pressure and high humidity makes us irritable. Studies have shown that certain kinds of winds can cause people to get ill, such as the hot, dry, gusty winds called *foehns* in the Alps in Europe and *chinooks* in the eastern Rockies. When the powerful wind called the *sharav* blows over Israel, it is blamed for headaches, upset stomachs, breathing problems, and irritable moods that affect 25 percent of the country's population! Although no one is certain why these winds affect people's health, some scientists think it may be a result of changes in the electrical properties of the air.

It's no mystery that we're happier and more calm when the weather is fair. So when the forecast calls for clear, sunny skies, it may be a good time to ask your parents for an **increase in your allowance!**

I hope you've enjoyed this journey into the amazing and wonderful world of weather. Now that you understand more about the water and wind systems, the clouds and the rain, and nature's awesome power, I hope you make a habit of watching the weather—in all its glory!

Glossary

air: a mixture of invisible molecules of nitrogen, oxygen, carbon dioxide, water vapor, and other substances.

abrasion: the process in which layers of soft rock are carried away by the wind, leaving only the hard rock behind.

air pressure: the weight of the atmosphere pressing down on the Earth.

anemometer: an instrument used to measure wind speed.

arctic: a cold climate.

atmosphere: the life-giving and protective layer of gases that surrounds Earth.

atom: the smallest unit of matter.

aurora australis: bands of light that appear over the southern regions of the Earth, caused by atomic particles hitting the Earth's magnetic field.

aurora borealis or **northern lights:** bands of light that appear over the northern regions of the Earth, caused by atomic particles hitting the Earth's magnetic field.

barometer: an instrument that measures air pressure.

blizzard: a severe winter storm that brings high winds, low temperatures, and blowing snow.

Celsius scale: a temperature scale in which 0 degrees is the freezing point of water and 100 degrees the boiling point of water.

cirrus: a cloud that forms in wispy strands high in the sky.

climate: the typical weather that occurs over a particular region of Earth.

cloud: a collection of water droplets or ice crystals in the atmosphere.

cloud seeding: a weather modification method in which chemicals are put into a cloud to make the cloud produce more precipitation.

condensation: the process of gas or vapor changing into a liquid.

convection current: the motion that occurs in liquids or gases of different temperatures.

Coriolis effect: a force that makes wind change direction, caused by Earth's rotation.

crystal: a solid made up of molecules that are neatly arranged in a precise, repeating pattern.

cumulus: a puffy white cloud formed by rising air heated by the sun.

current: a smooth flowing movement of air that flows up and down.

cyclone: a storm that spins around a low pressure area. Hurricanes, tornadoes, and typhoons are all types of cyclones.

depression: an area of low air pressure that usually brings unsettled weather.

desert: a region of Earth that has hot and dry weather throughout the year.

dew: moisture in the air that condenses on objects near or on the cooler surface of the Earth.

diameter: the distance through the center of an object, measured from one end to the other.

doldrums: currents of hot wind near the equator that flow almost straight upwards.

drizzle: very tiny drops of water that float to the ground.

drought: a prolonged period with little or no rainfall.

dust devils: rotating columns of air that can form in desert regions.

dust storm: high winds in dry weather that lift great amounts of dust into the air.

electron: a very small particle that carries a negative charge of electricity.

equator: the imaginary circle around the earth that divides the top half (Northern Hemisphere) from the bottom half (Southern Hemisphere).

exosphere: the outermost layer of the atmosphere surrounding Earth.

eye: the area of low pressure at the center of a hurricane, where the air is dry and calm.

eye wall: the band of clouds in a hurricane that surround the eye of the storm.

evaporation: the process in which liquid water changes into water vapor.

Fahrenheit scale: the temperature scale in which the freezing point of water is 32° and the boiling point of water is 212°.

fog: a collection of water droplets hanging close to the ground.

freezing rain: precipitation that falls as rain and freezes when it hits the ground or other surfaces.

front: an area in the atmosphere where cold and warm air systems meet.

glacier: a large mass of ice that forms when the climate is so cold that less snow melts in the summer than falls in the winter.

global warming: a gradual increase in the temperature of the earth due to the greenhouse effect.

gravity: a natural force that causes objects on the surface and in the atmosphere to be pulled toward the earth.

greenhouse effect: the filtering system in the atmosphere that prevents the Earth's warmth from escaping into space.

Gulf Stream: an ocean current in the Atlantic Ocean.

hail: ice balls that are formed by rain that is thrown by air currents back up into a thundercloud, where a layer of ice forms around it. Hail can make several trips back up into a cloud, where it is covered with another level of ice each time.

hailstreak: the path in which hail falls.

horizon: the line seen from a distance where the earth or sea seems to meet the sky.

horse latitudes: narrow bands of very weak winds surrounding the earth at about 30° north and south latitude.

humidity: the presence of water or water vapor in the air. When the weather is humid, there is a high amount of water in the air.

hurricane: the most severe type of tropical cyclone, with winds that spin around a low-pressure system.

hygrometer: an instrument used to measure relative humidity.

ice age: an extended period of time when a large portion of Earth's surface is covered by ice.

iceberg: a chunk of ice, usually broken off from a glacier, that floats in the ocean.

igloo: a house made of ice.

interglacial: the relatively warm period between ice ages.

intracloud lightning: lightning that occurs inside a cloud.

ion: an atom that carries an electric charge.

ionosphere: the layer of atmosphere that begins 50 miles (80 kilometers) above Earth and extends outward 300 miles (480 kilometers).

jet stream: a high-speed, narrow band of upper level winds that flows from west to east around the globe.

Kelvin scale: a temperature scale used by scientists in which "absolute zero" is −459.2° Fahrenheit.

leader: part of a lightning strike; the stream of ions flowing from the bottom of a cloud toward the ground.

lesser whirls: rotating pockets of air that do not get strong enough to become tornadoes.

lightning: a current of electricity that flows between clouds or between a cloud and the earth.

mesa: a mini-plateau, shaped by abrasion.

mesocyclone: a huge, spinning mass of air.

mist: a very thin layer of fog containing few water droplets.

Nor'easter: a storm that results when a low-pressure system moves up the east coast of the United States.

northern lights: see aurora borealis

plankton: tiny, single-celled plants and animals that live in the water and in the upper atmosphere.

plateau: a large, flat rock formation formed by wind erosion.

precipitation: any kind of rain or snow.

radiosonde: a package of meteorological instruments attached to a weather balloon.

rain gauge: the instrument meteorologists use to measure the amount of rainfall.

rainy reason: the month of heaviest rainfall that occur in a tropical climate.

refraction: the bending of light. Sunlight breaks into separate colors when it is bent.

relative humidity: the amount of water vapor in the air compared to the maximum amount of water vapor that air can possibly hold.

return stroke: the stream of ions flowing from the ground to a cloud that produces the bright flash in lightning.

sleet: precipitation that falls as tiny balls of ice.

snow crystals: objects formed in clouds that are colder than 32 degrees Fahrenheit.

spectrum: the series of colors seen when light is refracted, including violet, blue, green, yellow, orange, and red.

static electricity: a buildup of electric charge in an object that is insulated.

storm surge: the raised level of ocean water that surrounds a hurricane and causes much of the damage when a hurricane system hits land.

stratosphere: the layer of atmosphere that extends 6 to 50 miles (10 to 80 kilometers) above Earth.

stratus: horizontal layers of clouds that blanket the sky.

supercell thunderstorm: a powerful, long-lasting thunderstorm that can produce tornadoes.

temperate: a climate that has warm summers, cold winters, and rain and snow.

thermometer: an instrument used for measuring temperature.

thunder: sound waves created by the sudden increase in temperature in the air surrounding lightning.

thundershower: rain that falls on a particular area for a short amount of time.

tornado: a type of cyclone that is a violently rotating column of air extending from a thunderstorm to the ground.

tornado warning: an official notice that a tornado has been seen in the weather area.

tornado watch: an official notice that conditions are present for the formation of a tornado in the weather area.

trade winds: air that moves steadily toward the equator from an easterly direction.

tropical depression: a storm that forms over tropical waters with spinning winds that travel 38 miles per hour (61 km/hour) or less.

tropical storm: a storm that forms over tropical waters containing spinning winds that travel 39 to 74 miles per hour (62 to 119 km/hour).

tropics: the regions surrounding the north and south of the equator that receive the largest portion of the sun's energy.

troposphere: the layer of atmosphere in which weather occurs, extending from Earth's surface to 6 miles (10 kilometers) above the planet.

vortex: the spinning, central core of a tornado.

water cycle: the recycling system of Earth's water, in which water evaporates out of the oceans, forms clouds, falls as rain or snow, and drains back into the oceans through rivers.

waterspout: a tornado that touches down on water instead of land.

water vapor: water in gas form, created when liquid water evaporates.

weather: the condition of the atmosphere at a given time and place, including the temperature, wind speed, precipitation, and humidity.

weather modification: the process of using chemicals to change naturally occuring weather conditions.

wind: a smooth flowing movement of air that flows horizontally.

windchill: the colder temperature you feel when strong winds blow in cold temperatures.

Index